AF574741

# Down on the Farm

## The Down County Museum Farming Collection

Down Survey 2009

Yearbook of Down County Museum

**Editor:** M Lesley Simpson

Published by Down County Museum

# Down on the Farm

## Down Survey 2009

Yearbook of Down County Museum

**Editor:** M Lesley Simpson

**Photograph credits:**
Photography by Allen Thompson ABIPP, Down County Museum, or as credited, where the photographer is known; images from the museum collection unless otherwise stated.

All rights reserved. No part of this publication may be reproduced, stored in a retrieval system, or transmitted in any form by any means, electronic, mechanical, photocopying, recording or otherwise, without the prior written permission of the copyright owner and publisher of this book.

© Copyright Down County Museum and authors.

**ISBN** 9780337095689

The publication of this volume was generously supported by the Friends of Down County Museum. Members of the Friends will receive a free copy. Membership information is available from the museum at
The Mall, Downpatrick, County Down, BT30 6AH

**Telephone:** 028 4461 5218 **Fax:** 028 4461 5590 **Email:** museum@downdc.gov.uk

**Designed by LSD Ltd and printed by Graham & Heslip**

**Published by The Stationery Office**

**Front cover picture:** Harvest time in South Down, photographed by Pat Hudson. DCM H05/99/01/01

**Back cover picture:** Stewarts Motor Works, Downpatrick, celebrate the success of the Ferguson tractor. For more information see Chapter 2, Fig 8.

# Contents

Fig 1 Children with their pet lamb, on St Patrick's Drive, Downpatrick, 1970. The girl holding the lamb on a lead is Teresa Holland (DJ41/631/01).

# FOREWORD

This year's edition of the Down Survey is dedicated to one subject – farming in County Down. It marks another step forward in increasing access to our collection but is also the result of an enjoyable and fruitful partnership between two former members of staff of the Ulster Folk and Transport Museum, a former member of staff of the Ulster Museum and a former and present members of staff of Down County Museum. None of this would have been possible without the financial assistance of three organisations – The Northern Ireland Museums Council, the Museums Association and last but by no means least, the Friends of our own museum. The Northern Ireland Museums Council provided a grant towards fees and expenses for research provided by Jonathan Bell and Mervyn Watson and also for the publication of this book. The Museums Association, through a Monument Trust Fellowship, gave Brian Turner the opportunity to pass on information about objects and photographs relating to farming in our collection. The Friends provided the extra funds required to complete the whole project and for this, as always, we are very grateful. This is only the first part of Brian's contribution through his Fellowship – the second half will be spent on completing documentation of our unique collection of photographs taken by Tommy Gribben of Dinanew, Loughinisland and which was researched by Brian in his first few years at Down County Museum. His work on this will culminate in publication as the 2010 Down Survey.

Our farming related objects were collected largely during the 1980s, in the early stages of the museum development. It was felt necessary to make the collection at that time because many items were just about to disappear with the last of the 'horsepower' generation. Some of these objects gain their significance from particular local associations, such as a wooden plough from the Mournes, while others are rare survivals in a regional and even national context, for example County Down trottle cars. The invention of a County Down engineer, the Ferguson tractor and linkage system, revolutionised world farming so it is particularly fitting that we have one of his tractors in our museum. As a whole, the collection is significant as a record of the equipment used on a County Down farm from the late nineteenth to mid twentieth century. More importantly, when accompanied by images from our extensive photographic archive, the objects document the lives of farmers in our county. DJ McNeill's photographs (eg Figs 1-5 in this Foreword) are a particularly important resource.

Very few other local museums, and none in County Down, have collected this type of material. Elsewhere, other collections of this type are often left as a number of random objects which are not assessed and interpreted in relation to their particular area and circumstances. As our headquarters is based in an eighteenth century gaol there is no appropriate display space for such material within the current site, as it has been developed. The model farm in the country park at Delamont was identified some years ago as a more suitable option but these plans were not implemented. However, we do have the advantage, and potential, of a garden at the rear of the site where there is space to design and build a display gallery specifically for the most important objects in this collection. We hope that this book will demonstrate the significance of our collection and support the case for developing such a purpose built gallery for its permanent display. In the meantime, a temporary exhibition, open from December 2009 to April 2010 and organized in partnership with Monaghan County Museum, will provide a tantalizing glimpse of both objects and images.

The main purpose of the book, and proposed display space, is to increase access to our collection, interpret it and set it in its context. This is in line with our overall policy, Forward Plan and Collections Management Plan. As farming was, and still is, one of the main industries of County Down it is essential that this is properly recognised in our exhibitions and publications. There is still of course, great potential for more work in this

Fig 2 Ballydugan mill, derelict before its restoration by Noel Killen. The flour mill was built in 1792 by a company owned by John Aughinleck of Strangford (DJ41/877/01/01).

Fig 3 Farmers meeting on a country lane, probably near Ardglass. This is typical of D J McNeill's opportunistic photography – he didn't even stop to get out of the car but simply photographed his subjects through the windscreen! (DJ05/03/78/02).

area – researching the history of some of the farms mentioned in this book could be a substantial but rewarding exercise for the future.

M Lesley Simpson
December 2009

Fig 4 A student from Mr Keyes' Agricultural class at the Technical College, on a farm visit, 1981 (DJ48/02/46/06).

Fig 5 Students from the College on work experience in 1982, dipping sheep (DJ48/02/89/07). All photographs in this section by D J McNeill.

# CHAPTER 1

## Farming in County Down

Jonathan Bell and Mervyn Watson

During the last three centuries most farms in County Down have been very small - in the early nineteenth century many were less than five acres. Between 1750 and the mid-1840s, very tiny farms spread in hilly areas of the county, as poor people created holdings out of what had previously been waste land. The aim here was to secure a living for their families, and up to the Great Famine of the 1840s they were very successful in this, using the wonder crop of the age, the potato. In lowland areas, small farms spread with the development of the linen industry. Until the early nineteenth century, most linen was produced by farming families, who processed their flax crop, spun the linen thread, and wove it at home. This system of linen production was very labour intensive, well suited to small farms and big families. In the early nineteenth century, linen production moved into factories and many of the small farms were no longer viable. However, even after more than one hundred years, the impact of the linen industry meant that the average size of farms in County Down in 1957 was thirty to fifty acres.[1] By contrast, elsewhere in Ireland most landlords resisted subdivision on good land, allowing it on marginal areas, which were largely cleared by the Famine and its aftermath.

Within this overall pattern of small mixed farms, there was a lot of variety in farming within County Down. By the early twentieth century, for example, the area around Belfast had farms specialising in dairying, while the northern part of the Ards peninsula, with its relatively dry climate, was known for vegetable production. The Ards and the coastal areas of Mourne, with their sandy soils and plentiful supplies of seaweed for fertiliser, had become centres of excellence for potato cultivation.[2] By contrast, the hill farms of the Mourne Mountains in the south of the county were known for sheep farming.[3]

From the eighteenth century onwards, Irish farming methods were recorded in increasing detail, and some of the best early evidence comes from County Down. For example, our clearest surviving illustration of an Old Irish long-beamed plough, one of the 'common' ploughs of the period, comes from near Hillsborough (Fig1). However, the county was also in the forefront of improved farming. For example, a Mr Christy of Kirkassock near Magheralin, claimed to be the first farmer to have installed a threshing machine in Ireland, in 1796,[4] and County Down farmers were involved in early experiments in the development of horse-drawn reaping machines. A machine demonstrated to a number of gentlemen in 1806 at a specially arranged event in Moira, for example, was one of the earliest such events in Ireland.[5] The small commercial farms that were common throughout the county adopted a lot of the new foundry-produced equipment from the early nineteenth century onwards. These standardised, mass-produced implements are the main evidence of horse-powered farm machinery within County Down.

Fig 1 Ploughing near Hillsborough in 1783. The 'common' wooden plough is pulled by four native ponies known as 'garrons'. The collars and other parts of harness shown are made of twisted straw known as *súgán.* (W Hincks, Courtesy of the Linenhall Library, Belfast).

Fig 2 A Ferguson tractor reaping grain in 1938. (Courtesy of the Museum of Rural Life, Reading).

In the twentieth century, a County Down man, Harry Ferguson, was responsible for Ireland's most celebrated contribution to the development of farm machinery, the Ferguson tractor with its three point linkage and hydraulic lift (Fig 2). The Ferguson system allowed farmers to control implements attached to the back of the tractor, raising or lowering them, or moving them sideways as they drove. This transformed the tractor from an unwieldy 'iron horse' into the main source of power in crop production. Tractors incorporating the system were manufactured in 1936, and by the 1950s, the 'Wee Grey Fergie' was world famous.

## Crops

During the last three hundred years, the main crops grown in County Down were potatoes, oats and hay. Oats have been grown here for thousands of years, while potatoes became the staple crop for most Irish people during the seventeenth century. A reference to potato growing near Comber in 1606 may not be substantiated but by the 1680s, potatoes were said to have become 'the chief article of food' of the 'common' people all over the country.[6] Hay was not widely grown in Ireland before the eighteenth century, but after the Famine of the 1840s, there was a long-term swing away from crops to livestock, and by 1900 hay was the biggest crop after pasture.[7]

Most farm crops in Ireland are cultivated annually, and the first task is to till or turn the ground. This was done with spades and ploughs. Irish farmers are said to be the best spadesmen in the world. By the early nineteenth century, hundreds of different types of spades were used, often to make cultivation ridges, the dimensions of which could be varied to suit the soil, slope, aspect, crop grown, and season of planting.[8] In Ulster most of these spades were made in spade mills. The main mills in County Down were in Newtown townland in the parish of Kilbroney, or nearby in the parish of Newry, in the townlands of Finnard, Damolly,

**The Improved Field Spade for Manual Labour.**

THE SUBSCRIBER begs to direct the attention of Landlords, Farmers, and Agriculturists to the IMPROVED FIELD SPADE so much approved of by the Royal Agricultural Improvement Society of Ireland, and the Royal Dublin Society, as being the best implement for the prosecution of Spade Husbandry, and recommended by the Society's Practical Instructor, Mr. Quinn, for its cheapness and great advantage in agriculture.

Persons desirous of obtaining the Improved Spade, can be supplied on application at the Manufacturer's sole Agents' in Dublin, Messrs. WM. DRUMMOND and SONS, Seedsmen, 58, Dawson-street, and Mr. JOHN MAGUIRE'S, 10, Dawson-street; or in NEWRY, at the maker's Foundry, who is the original manufacturer of this useful implement.

FRANCIS CARVILL.

Newry, Jan. 16, 1850.

☞ Specimens of this implement can be seen at the office of the Secretary to the Royal Agricultural Improvement Society of Ireland, 41, Upper Sackville-street, or at the Royal Dublin Society's Agricultural Museum, Kildare-street, and its advantages explained by the Curator.

CASH PRICE

Men's Spades, 20s. per dozen........1s. 10d. each.
Boys' Spades, 18s. per dozen........1s. 8d. each.

Fig 3 An advertisement for Carvill of Newry, published in *The Irish Farmers Gazette* in 1850.

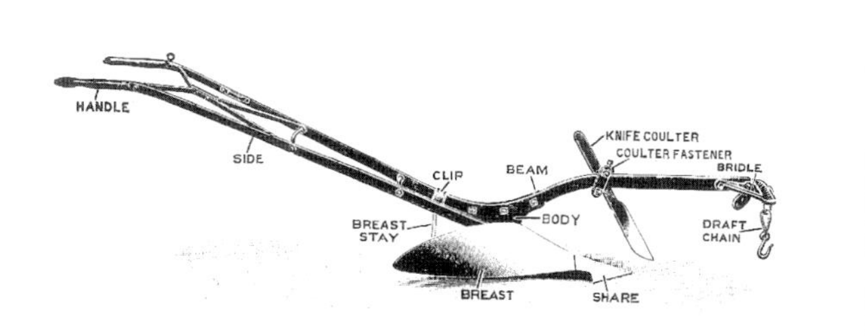


Fig 4 Scottish swing plough.

and Newry town. The Newry firm of Carvill was the first to manufacture an 'improved' type of spade that was quickly adopted throughout the east of Ireland (Fig 3).[9]

From the mid-1700s farming publications were full of discussions about the potential of improved implements and methods. County Down farmers were very quick to adopt these new developments, once their usefulness and reliability were demonstrated. In the early nineteenth century, for example, most farmers in the county began to use Scottish 'swing' ploughs (Fig 4). Like the Old Irish ploughs these had no wheels, but unlike the older ploughs, they were made of metal and were designed so that they could be pulled by two horses, and turn sods so that these lay in even furrow slices. These ploughs remained popular, especially in hillier areas, until well into the twentieth century. It was only after land had been well-drained and levelled that farmers began to use English style wheel or 'chill' ploughs, which can still be seen in use at several annual ploughing matches within the county (Fig 5).

One of the main achievements of the early period of experimentation and debate, was the development of drill cultivation of crops. The idea behind making drills is simple. Drills are long, straight equidistant rows, and crops grown in them can be sown, cared for, and harvested more methodically than crops sown broadcast.

Fig 5 A wheel plough in use on Edward Rea's farm at Annacloy, in the 1940s -1950s. The ploughman is Mr Daniel Marner, and the plough is now in the collection of Down County Museum. (plough DCM 1984-8; photo DCM 05/35/09)

The great champion of drill cultivation in England was Jethro Tull, who developed a machine for sowing grain crops in drills in the early eighteenth century. In Ireland, implements for making drills were being manufactured as early as the 1760s, but the drill cultivation of grain was mostly found on larger farms. However, by the 1830s, farmers in most parts of the country were growing potatoes in 'raised' drills. These were made in soil that had already been ploughed, and loosened by harrowing. Special 'drill ploughs' were then used to push the soil into low triangular ridges. Potatoes were planted in the furrows between these, and the drill plough was then drawn up through the middle of each ridge, to push the soil over the seed. The earliest illustration of a drill plough that we know of in Ireland was published in a book about County Down, in 1802 (Fig 6).[10]

Farmers in the Mourne area also developed their own ingenious modification of older wooden ploughs, so that they could be used to make drills. A block of wood, known as a 'false reest' was attached to the flat 'land' side of the plough. This created a two-sided plough that could be used to push soil into drills. These dual-purpose ploughs were used in the Mournes well into the twentieth century (Fig 7). Later Mourne ploughs were used only to make drills, but their early history as ploughs used for turning furrows could still be seen in their asymmetrical construction.

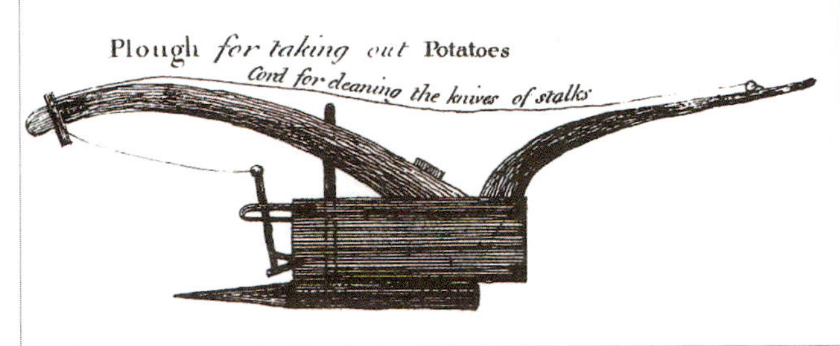


Fig 6 Wooden drill plough, illustrated in Dubordieu, John *A Statistical Survey of County Down* (Dublin, 1802), p52.

Fig 7 Hugh Chambers of Moneydarragh, demonstrating the use of a Mourne plough in the 1970s. (© Jonathan Bell and Mervyn Watson).

Growing potatoes and other root crops in drills meant that weeding of growing crops could be mechanised. Because the crops were spaced equally apart, it was possible for horse-drawn weeding implements to be pulled along the rows. Grubbers are fitted with iron feet, and these pulled out weeds growing between the rows, without damaging the growing potatoes. A drill plough could then be pulled between the drills, pushing earth up over the potato plants, to give more soil for the development of tubers. Horse-drawn machines for harvesting potatoes could also be used when the crop was grown in drills. These implements had a blade that cut under the potatoes, and spinning metal forks, or feet, which knocked the tubers out of the ground. One of the earliest effective potato digging machines was patented by a County Antrim man in 1855.[11]

By the mid nineteenth century, the harvesting of grain was becoming mechanised successfully. In1852 American reaping machines were shown at the Royal Ulster Agricultural Show in Belfast, and farmers quickly became aware of the potential of the new machines. In 1858, trials at Clandeboye in North Down led some 'gentlemen' farmers present to claim that the reaper-mower manufactured by the English firm of Burgess and Key performed best at harvesting both oats and hay.[12] The history of Irish farming is notable for the extent to which very old techniques can co-exist with modern ones. For example, on at least one large farm in County Down, Maxwell's at Finnebrogue, oxen were used as draught animals until well into the twentieth century.[13] More often, however, the use of older techniques was associated with small scale farming. For example, while commercial farmers were buying horse drawn reaping machines, many small hill farmers were still using sickles to harvest their grain. This was not because they were in some way irrationally conservative, but because they understood which farming methods suited their scale of crop production, and available labour. Using a sickle is very labour intensive. The reaper using a sickle holds each handful of grain stalks as he, or she, cuts through them. Sickle blades have serrated edges, and the grain is cut with a sawing motion. This method of harvesting has big advantages. Because each handful of grain is cut individually, grain that has been flattened by wind or rain can be lifted up and cut. Also, the reaper selects which stalks to cut, so that weeds growing among the crop can be left behind. Finally, because each handful is held, the grain heads are not badly shaken while being harvested and seed is not lost. This was a particularly important advantage in the mild, damp Irish climate, where grain took longer to ripen, and seed was more likely to be loosened in the grain heads.

The skill with which Irish harvesters could reap with sickles meant that harvest workers, who travelled to Britain for seasonal work, were in big demand, so much so that they slowed up the introduction of the scythe to parts of Britain.[14] The late Joey Murphy, whose family had a farm in the Glen, near Hilltown, recorded an account of a scythe being demonstrated in the Mournes by a returning migrant worker in the later nineteenth century. Using a scythe to cut grain was a novelty, and a lot of local people came to watch the demonstration (Fig 8).[15]

Scythes, probably introduced by the Anglo-Normans in the twelfth century, were also used for mowing grass to make hay. By 1900, hay was the biggest crop in Ireland, but by this time the introduction of horse drawn reaping machines was well under way. The production of grass seed was well established in the early twentieth century. By the 1960s, County Down produced half the rye grass seed grown in Ulster (Fig 9).[16]

Fig 8 Mowing grain with a scythe. This is a rare illustration of a simple 'cradle' fixed to the back of the scythe, to catch the harvested grain neatly as it fell. The scythesman was probably Barney Sloane, and the photograph was taken by Pat Hudson at Lisnaree in Glenloughan. (DCM H05/67/01)

Fig 9 Mowing rye grass. Grass grown for hay should be cut before the seed ripens, but in the early twentieth century, the cultivation of grass for seed became important in Ulster. County Down produced half of the rye grass seed grown commercially. Photograph by DJ McNeill. (DCM DJ05/43/03/07)

## Livestock

Before tractors became common in the 1950s, manual labour and horses were the main sources of power

Fig.10 William Lyons of Gannoway with two of his daughters, Dolly and Isabel, in 1933. The horse on the left is a 'clean bone', purchased from a local bakery. (Courtesy of Dolly McRoberts).

on farms. As in the rest of Ireland, horses in County Down were often used for a range of tasks - tillage, driving and riding. This meant that they tended to be smaller than horses used only for farm work. In the eighteenth century, most farmers used 'garrons', small, sturdy working horses (Fig 1). In the next hundred years, selective breeding led to the spread of larger working horses, but these still tended to be smaller than English or continental breeds. They were also mostly 'clean boned', with slender legs and small feet (Fig 10). Most farmers preferred these qualities, because the horses could work more neatly, for instance when ploughing; their small feet meant that they could step neatly along the line of a furrow. Some North Down farmers used heavier Clydesdale horses, for extra pulling power. Clydesdale breeders in the county developed a good reputation, especially in the 1980s and subsequently, when the quality of Clydesdales bred in Ulster rivalled that of Scotland, where the breed originated.

Tractors began to displace horses on County Down farms during the Second World War and by 1960 working horses were becoming uncommon.

| County Down | 1939 | 1959 |
|---|---|---|
| Horses | 27,159 | 2,300 |
| Tractors | 140 | 7,750[17] |

Apart from horses, numbers of livestock in County Down have grown almost continuously since the mid nineteenth century. During the eighteenth and mid nineteenth centuries, cattle in the county were kept for both meat and milk. This was particularly the case on small hill farms in the south of the county. Several attempts were made by breeders in nineteenth century Ireland to develop a useful 'dual-purpose' breed of cattle for small farms on marginal land. Some landlords took an interest in promoting specific breeds. In the late nineteenth century, for example, the Countess of Clanwilliam kept a herd of Kerry cattle on the Montalto estate in Ballynahinch.[18] In Ulster generally, some breeders worked at the establishment of the Irish Moiled cattle breed. These cattle shared characteristics, such as colouring, with animals described in ancient literature, but the breed society was not established successfully until 1926. 'Moilie' cattle flourished on a small scale during the 1930s, but then went into a slow decline. By 1982, one of only two herds in the world survived on the farm of Mr Jimmy Nelson outside Killyleagh. This herd was used to re-establish the cattle as a highly valued rare breed (Fig 11).

Fig 11 Irish Moiled cattle at the Ulster Folk and Transport Museum, Cultra, County Down. (© Jonathan Bell and Mervyn Watson).

In North Down, the demands of Belfast for dairy produce led to the development of specialised dairy farming, and by 1900 the main breed here, as elsewhere in Northern Europe, was the Dairy Shorthorn (Fig12). Throughout the county as a whole Shorthorns and Aberdeen Angus were the most common breeds.[19]

Pigs were kept on most small County Down farms. By the early nineteenth century, Ulster farmers had crossed native Irish Greyhound pigs with improved Dutch and Berkshire breeds, to develop their own distinctive Large White Ulster pig, which was formally established as a breed in 1907[20] (Fig.13). It was claimed that 'for

Fig 12 Cattle on the Fair Green in Downpatrick photographed by D J McNeill. Most of the cattle seem to be of a Shorthorn type. (DCM DJ05/41/312/01)

Fig 13 A Large White Ulster pig at a fair in Castlewellan c1910. (Ulster Folk and Transport Museum WAG 1175, Courtesy of the Trustees National Museums Northern Ireland).

Fig 14 Slaughtered pigs with their innards removed, photographed by Tommy Gribben. (DCM G05/87/14/241)

early maturity and economy of production, high class flavour and quality of bacon' the Large White Ulster was unsurpassed.[21] The Large White Ulster was also thin-skinned, however, which meant that live pigs could be easily bruised while being moved. This meant that until the mid twentieth century, pigs in Ulster tended to be slaughtered on the farm (Fig 14). Large White Ulster pigs declined in numbers during the 1930s, as tastes changed to leaner meat, and the establishment of pork-curing plants set up as part of the Pig Marketing Scheme in 1933 led to pigs being taken away from farms for slaughtering. By the 1960s, the breed was extinct.[22]

Sheep, like other livestock, increased greatly in numbers in the lowlands of County Down from the mid nineteenth century (Fig 15). However, the most distinctive type of sheep in the county were found in the Mountains of Mourne (Fig16). Mourne sheep were recognised as distinctive as early as 1802, when they were described as 'very finely made in all points, finely woolled and much prized for … mutton'.[23] Critics have claimed that Mourne sheep are inferior versions of Scottish Blackface sheep, but farmers in Mourne have continued to argue that they are superior, in size, hardiness and quality, and attempts are under way to get formal recognition for them.[24]

## Fairs, Markets and Marts

Markets and fairs were the main means of trade for many rural people until well into the twentieth century. Markets depended on a regular (usually weekly) flow of trade, whereas fairs were seasonal or monthly, and more specialised. However, there was a large overlap in the activities carried on at both types of event.

Markets were held in many County Down towns. Downpatrick market, for example, was held every

Fig 15 A flock of sheep at Ballydugan, photographed by D J McNeill. (DCM DJ05/41/857/03)

Fig 16 Flock of Mourne sheep near Spelga photographed by D J McNeill. (DCM DJ05/75/26/01)

Fig 17 A linen fair in Banbridge, in 1783. (W Hincks, courtesy of the Linenhall Library, Belfast)

Saturday, and in the 1830s and 1840s it was described as well supplied with provisions of all kinds.[25] By this time also, several ports in the county were exporting agricultural produce. From the Downpatrick area, wheat, barley, oats cattle, pigs and potatoes were exported from the Quoile quay, and from Newcastle, oats, barley and potatoes, 'of which large quantities are sent to Dublin and Liverpool.'[26]

Fairs (Irish: *aonaighe*) were an important part of early Irish society, often associated with a saint's pattern, or other important ritual occasion. The Anglo-Normans established fairs primarily as commercial events, and patents to hold fairs were granted as part of this development. By the seventeenth century, towns such as Ballynahinch had regular fairs; by the 1830s, fairs were held in the town on the first Thursday of every month apart from June, September, and December.[27] By the later eighteenth century, many County Down towns had fairs associated with the sale of brown linens (Fig17). The situation in Banbridge in the 1830s shows how well-developed the organisation of fairs and markets could be by this time.

> The town … has risen … to an eminent degree of commercial importance as the head of the principal district of linen manufacture … The market house [is] situated in the centre of the town … a large and handsome edifice surmounted by a dome and built by the Marquee [sic] of Downshire in 1834, at an expense of £2,000. A brown linen hall was also erected by him in 1817, and a market-place for meal and grain in 1817, and held on the first Monday in every month; and fairs for horses, cattle, sheep, pigs, and manufactured goods, are held on Jan 12th, first Saturday in March, June 9th, August 26th, and November 16th; the last is a very noted fair for horses.[28]

Fairs remained an important part of the economic life of Banbridge and other towns such as Rathfriland, Downpatrick and Saintfield well into the 1950s (Fig 18).

Hiring fairs, for the recruitment of farm servants, were well established by the late nineteenth century. At least ten towns in County Down had hiring fairs.[29] They were usually held twice a year, in May and November. Servants looking for work would gather at a central place in the town, where they would bargain with prospective employers, mostly local farmers. The servant would usually live on the farm for six months, receiving bed and board, and a small monetary payment at the end of the term.

Fairs in general were organised to meet the changing needs of regions within the county. For example, in 1837, the main fairs in Hilltown were for linen yarn and cattle.[30] At this time, the nearby uplands of the Mourne mountains were used as summer pastures for cattle. Later in the century, however, sheep numbers began to increase very rapidly, and by the 1880s, sheep rather than cattle were kept on the mountains. In the twentieth century, the Mournes were nearly all common grazing for sheep.[31] The fairs in Hilltown reflected this development, and the best known fairs, held in August, September and October, were for the sale of sheep (Fig.19). At the 'Tup Fair' in September, as late as the 1970s, a ram was brought on to stage at a dance organised on the evening

Fig 18 The horse fair at Banbridge, photographed by Pat Hudson in 1944. (DCM H05/12/01)

Fig 19 A sheep fair at Hilltown, photographed by D J McNeill. (DCM DJ05/89/02)

of the fair. The festive aspect of the event became its core when the event was re-organised as the 'Boley Fair' in 1986. In the 1950s, the biggest monthly fairs in County Down were held in Ballynahinch, Rathfriland and Crossgar.[32] However, by this time, fairs began to be replaced by marts and auctions: formal auctions were held regularly in a purpose-built yard and sales ring. These are now the main local centres for livestock trade throughout the county (Fig 20).

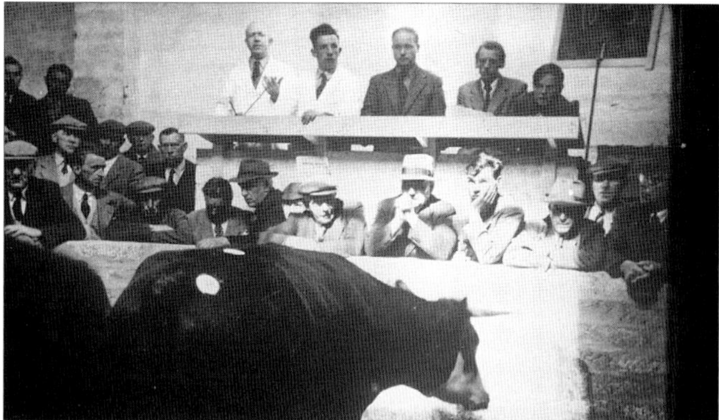

Fig 20 The cattle mart at Downpatrick, photographed by D J McNeill. The auctioneer in the photograph has been identified as Mr George Press, and the clerk as Jack Hutton. The two men on the left of Mr Hutton are Ministry of Agriculture officials. The other is possibly Jack Hamill. (DCM DJ05/41/06/03)

**Recent History**

The thirty years following the Second World War were a time of relative security for County Down farmers. The war had entrenched the notion that government had a direct role to play in guaranteeing agricultural markets, so farmers could be assured of minimum prices for their produce. Numbers of livestock (cattle, pigs and poultry) in the county have increased steadily since the war. Crop production declined, but investment in modern machinery continued. For example, by 1960 there were 200 combine harvesters in the county, half the total number in Northern Ireland.[33] The number of farmers declined, but farm size increased, from around 50 acres in the 1950s, to 90.64 acres (36.7 hectares) in 2007.[34]

The security of County Down farmers came under threat during the 1980s, when the European Union began the slow, painful task of dismantling the Common Agricultural Policy. By the end of the 1990s, farming had become much more risky, and many farms were no longer operated on a full-time basis. However, in the first ten years of the new millennium, things have changed again. The development of bio-fuels, and increased demands for grain have meant that prices have risen, and for the first time in decades the acreages of crops have increased. It remains to be seen if this heralds a new era of prosperity for County Down farmers.

## REFERENCES

[1] Symons, *Leslie Land Use in Northern Ireland* (London: University of London Press, 1963), p 45.
[2] Davidson, W D 'Successful Potato Growing' Department of Agriculture and Technical Instruction for Ireland *Journal* vol 22 (Dublin, 1922), pp 140 – 145.
[3] Mogey, John M *Rural Life in Northern Ireland* (London: Oxford University Press, 1947), p 23.
[4] Bell, J and Watson, M *A History of Irish Farming 1750 – 1950* (Dublin: Four Courts Press, 2008), p 203.
[5] Ibid, p 190.
[6] Salaman, R N 'The Influence of the Potato on the Course of Irish History' (Dublin: The Tenth Finlay Memorial Lecture, Dublin, 1944), p 17.
[7] Department of Agriculture and Technical Instruction for Ireland 'Haymaking' Leaflet no 46 *Journal* vol 4 (Dublin, HMSO, 1904), p 716.
[8] Bell, J and Watson, M op cit, p 88.
[9] Watson, Mervyn 'Spades Versus Ploughs: A Nineteenth Century Debate: Part 2' *Ulster Folklife* vol 49 (Belfast, 2004).
[10] Dubordieu, John *A Statistical Survey of the County of Down* (Dublin, 1802), p 52.
[11] Bell, J and Watson, M op cit, p 148.
[12] Ibid, p 190.
[13] Donovan, Jack 'The Odd Couple', correspondence to *The Heavy Horse Magazine*, vol 12:1 (1998), p 54.
[14] Ibid, pp 186-187.
[15] Ibid.
[16] Symons, Leslie 'The Agricultural Industry 1921 -1962' in Symons, Leslie *Land Use in Northern Ireland* (London: University of London Press, 1963), p 49.
[17] Gillespie, J 'County Down in the Van of Progress' Government of Northern Ireland, Ministry of Agriculture *Monthly Report* vol 34 (HMSO: 1960), pp 263.
[18] Bell, J and Watson, M. op cit p 234.
[19] Government of Northern Ireland, Ministry of Agriculture *Monthly Report* vol 10 (April 1936) (HMSO: Belfast, 1936), p 9
[20] Ibid, pp 268-269.
[21] Coey, W E 'The Pig in Ireland' in A E Muskett (ed) *A A McGuckian: A Memorial Volume* (Belfast, 1956), p 61.
[22] Bell, J and Watson, M op cit, pp 270-271
[23] Dubordieu, John *A Statistical Survey of the County of Down* (Dublin, 1802), p 302.
[24] Bell, J and Watson, M op cit, pp 253-255
[25] Lewis, Samuel op cit, vol 2, p 493; *The Parliamentary Gazetteer of Ireland* vol 11 (Dublin: Fullerton, 1846), p 61
[26] Lewis, Samuel, op cit, vol 2 pp 424 and 493.
[27] Lewis, Samuel *A Topographical Dictionary of Ireland* vol.1 (London: Lewis, 1837), p 108.
[28] Ibid, p 177
[29] Hiring fairs were held in Ballynahinch, Ballywalter, Banbridge, Castlewellan, Comber, Downpatrick, Killyleagh, Kircubbin, Newtownards and Rathfriland. The biggest fair serving the county was held in Newry. O'Dowd, Anne *Spalpeens and Tattie Hokers* (Dublin: Irish Academic Press, 1991), pp 105-107.
[30] Ibid, vol 2 , p 5.
[31] Boal, F W 'County Down' in Symons, op cit., p.230.
[32] Government of Northern Ireland, Ministry of Agriculture *Monthly Report* vol.25 (HMSO: Belfast, 1951)
[33] Gillespie, J. op cit, p163.
[34] Agricultural Census of Northern Ireland, 2007.

# CHAPTER 2

## The Down County Museum Photographic Archive

Jonathan Bell and Mervyn Watson

There are several hundred photographs in the archives of Down County Museum which relate to farming. A small selection is illustrated here, showing the range and richness of the subjects covered. Of those included, several were taken by D J McNeill (1906-1988), of Dundrum and later Downpatrick, others by Tommy Gribben (1882-1959), of Loughinisland, the late Eric Malone of Downpatrick and Pat Hudson, formerly of Kilkeel. However, there are also a number of images, copied from old prints, which were taken by unknown photographers, and lent by members of our community, which provide a unique resource for the history of County Down.

**Fig 1 Ploughing with horses (H05/69/07)**

Farmers ploughed land throughout the year, but mostly in autumn and spring. From the mid nineteenth century, most ground was ploughed in sections known as 'flats', each about 20-30 feet across. The central furrows were turned first, and provided a guide line for horses and ploughman. The horses walked up one side of the flat, and down the other. This photograph was taken by Pat Hudson of Kilkeel, probably at Killowen or Ballyedmond, in 1942. Carlingford Lough is in the background.

**Fig 2 Ploughing lesson (DJ48/02/374/02)**

Until the 1950s there were more horses used on County Down farms than tractors. This photograph, taken by D J McNeill in 1955, shows students in an agriculture class from Downpatrick Technical College receiving practical instruction in ploughing. In the background is Down High School, where Technical College classes were then held, and a Nissen hut, which was probably erected during the Second World War.

**Fig 3 Planting potatoes in drills, using a horse and a bullock (05/61/49)**

On small farms, only one horse might be kept. Farmers often made up a two-horse plough team by borrowing a horse from a neighbour. Where this was not possible, a cow or bullock might be harnessed to the plough, as here on James Boyd's farm at Ballyglighorn near Killinchy around 1960. Where farmers used these mixed teams over a long period, they usually sold the bullock after three years and trained another one.

**Fig 4 Planting potatoes in drills (05/35/28)**
Mr J McClurg is planting potatoes on the farm of Mr H Matthews at Ballygally. From the 1830s, most potatoes grown in Ireland were planted in long, straight, raised rows or drills. This made planting, weeding and harvesting easier. This photograph was taken by Eric Malone, between 1959 and 1962.

**Fig 5 Weeding turnips (DCM 05/35/32)**

Turnips were, like potatoes, mostly grown in drills. Even where weeding was not mechanised, it was made easier by the regular spacing of the drills. This photograph shows the Calvert family and others weeding a field of turnips grown in the early 1950s to raise funds for the new Methodist church and manse in Downpatrick. The turnips were grown in a field owned by Nelson Calvert of Dunanelly, who is on the right of the photograph, beside the Rev Samuel McCaffrey.

**Fig 6 Rolling a field (G05/87/44)**
Rolling breaks up lumps of earth, and compacts it. It also flattens the ground, making care of growing crops and harvesting easier. This photograph was taken by Tommy Gribben on the family farm at Dinanew, Loughinisland. Although this isn't technically a good photograph it is a rare image of a roller in use.

**Fig 7 A blacksmith's forge in 1908 (05/73/28)**

Blacksmiths could repair most horse-operated farm implements, and also construct them, often using parts obtained from a local foundry. This photograph of Bryansford forge is copied from a postcard – the halfpenny stamp was cancelled 'Bryansford Co Down 5.30pm March 6th 1908'. At that time John Peters, second from the right, was the village blacksmith and coach builder, employing sixteen men. The smithy has since been demolished and replaced by a bungalow.

**Fig 8 Stewart's Motor Works (DJ05/41/1009/01)**
The advent of internal combustion engines and tractors marked the end of a lot of implement making and farriery for most blacksmiths. Many diversified, and became expert in repairing engines. After the Second World War, most forges were replaced by specialist garages. This photograph, taken outside Stewart's Motor Works on St Patrick's Avenue, Downpatrick, celebrates the triumph of Ferguson's tractors. Stewart's had started life as a blacksmith's forge, from which the museum holds a selection of tools.

**Fig 9 An early tractor (05/63/42)**

This photograph was taken on Island Taggart in 1919. The tractor was probably a Fordson and thought to be the first in this area. Before Harry Ferguson's revolutionary tractor designs, most farmers did not see tractors as useful for cultivation work. They were relatively unmanageable, operating as a very heavy 'iron horse,' which compacted soil and made it harder to drain and work. At the end of the First World War in 1918, there were only 640 tractors in the whole of Ireland.

**Fig 10 Planting potatoes using a tractor and converted trottle car (05/35/24)**
Farmers converted many horse-drawn implements for use with a tractor. This photograph, taken by Eric Malone in 1959 on Mr H Matthews' farm at Ballygally, near Downpatrick, shows seed potato being unloaded from a trottle car that has been fitted with pneumatic wheels and a draw bar.

**Fig 11 Planting potatoes using a tractor (DJ05/03/78/02)**
By the 1970s, tractors had become the everyday source of power on most County Down farms. This photograph was taken by D J McNeill about 1978 in the Long Field, in Ross townland, near Ardglass. Patrick William Connor is driving a Massey Ferguson 35 tractor and his children, Patrick Junior, Niall, Jarlath, Carmel and Edel, are helping to plant seed potatoes. Patrick Junior is holding a 'rubber' (possibly Ulster-Scots derivation, for an improvised apron made from coarse material) of seed potatoes – this was an old meal bag tied around the waist like an apron and then the end was gathered up to make a receptacle for holding the potatoes.

**Fig 12 A Ferguson tractor in 1980 (DJ05/73/61/18)**
Tractors became increasingly important for farmers after the end of the Second World War in 1945. By the late 1970s, work with heavy horses had almost disappeared except as a leisure activity in events such as ploughing matches. This photograph of a float celebrating the importance of Ferguson tractors, was taken by D J McNeill at a parade in Newcastle in 1980. Note the lorry at the front is from Stewart's Motor Works (see Fig 8).

**Fig 13 Steeping flax (05/44/06)**

The cultivation of flax and the home production of linen had a major effect on farm size in County Down, but by the early twentieth century very little flax was grown in Ulster. There was a rapid expansion of flax cultivation during the two World Wars, but by the 1950s, the crop had almost entirely disappeared. This photograph was taken during a project organised by Mr Richard McConville, who owned a scutch mill near Dromore. The men in the photograph are Mr McConville's sons. Flax is steeped for one or two weeks after it is pulled, to rot or 'ret' the wooden central part of the flax stem, so that it can be separated from the valuable fibre surrounding it. This photograph was taken at Ballyvicnakelly on 23rd August 1982.

**Fig 14 Haymaking (05/35/26)**
Hay was the most widely cultivated crop on County Down farms throughout most of the twentieth century. After cutting, the hay has to be frequently turned to assist drying. This photograph was taken by Eric Malone on the farm of Mr H Matthews at Ballygally, between 1959-1962. The woman is very elegantly dressed for haymaking!

**Figure 15 A haylifter (05/46/07)**

Haylifters were flat-bottomed carts, which had a winching mechanism fitted at the front. The body of the cart could be tilted so that the back touched the ground. Large ricks (or rucks) of hay could then be winched on the cart. This photograph was taken at Leverogue in the mid 1930s. The people are:

Back (left to right) Victor Marshall, Denis Marshall, Elizabeth Waterworth, David Marshall, Adam Marshall and David Marshall junior. Front (left to right) Adam Marshall junior, Agnes Marshall and Minnie Marshall.

**Fig 16 Harvesting potatoes (DJ05/41/858/01)**

This photograph of Cotter's Field, Quarter Cormick, shows about twenty six, mostly young people, engaged in lifting potatoes that have been knocked out of opened drills using a mechanical digger. Although partly mechanised, lifting the potatoes was still backbreaking work. Until the 1960s, many schools in County Down gave pupils a week off in autumn, for potato harvesting. The photograph was taken by D J McNeill, probably between about 1975 and 1985. The farm in the background belonged to the Thompson family but this field had been 'taken' by a farmer called Mr McGloo, who was known locally as 'one of the Mourne men'. The potato gatherers may include family members and seasonal recruits.

**Fig 17 Harvesting potatoes (G05/87/14)**
The horse-drawn potato digger can be seen on the right of this photograph, on the farm of Hugh Smyth of Magheratimpany, near Ballynahinch. The photograph was taken by Tommy Gribben in the late 1940s.

**Fig 18 Reaping grain (05/35/15)**

Reaping machines became common on County Down farms during the late nineteenth century. The machines cut the grain very quickly, but to take advantage of the increased rate of cutting, more people were required to bind the sheaves. This photograph was taken at the Mullagh, near Killyleagh, probably in the early twentieth century. The man on the left is thought to be Thomas Robinson. The image is one of several from this area copied for the museum archive from glass half plates.

**Fig 19 Fixing a horse's shoe (05/63/44)**
Horses' feet are very delicate, and constant attention is needed to keep them in good condition. This horse is harnessed to a reaping machine. The sheaf board, which collected newly cut sheaves of grain can be seen in the foreground of the photograph, which was taken on Breeze's farm at Ballymacromwell. Mr Breeze is the man seated on the right.

**Fig 20 Reaper binder (DJ05/68/01/02)**

The American firm McCormick's began to produce reaper-binders commercially in 1887. These machines had the big advantage that they not only cut, but tied sheaves of grain, a big saving of labour. This photograph, taken at Loughbrickland in 1913, is unusual, as many farmers at this time did not believe the investment in these expensive, complex machines was justified. The government's compulsory tillage policies during the First World War changed this, and many farmers either bought or hired a reaper-binder during the grain harvest. The photograph was copied from an early print by D J McNeill.

Fig 21 Stack yard (G05/87/45)
After grain had been reaped and stooked to dry, it was moved to a stack yard, or haggard, until the seed could be removed by threshing. This could be done over the winter, using flails or threshing machines. Hay stacks were also stored in the haggard. This stackyard was photographed by Tommy Gribben.

**Fig 22 Threshing grain using steam power (05/35/12)**

Portable threshing machines were used in Ireland from the 1850s. The machines were too expensive for most farmers to buy, so they were hired for one or more days, which meant that all the grain on the farm could be threshed at one time. Up to fourteen men were required to operate the machines, and farmers used the help of neighbours to make up the team. Neighbours would move around from farm to farm during threshing time. Most early machines were powered by a steam traction engine, as here at a farm at the Mullagh, near Killyleagh. This image probably dates from the late nineteenth or very early twentieth century and was copied from a glass half plate.

**Fig 23 Threshing grain using a tractor (DJ05/43/03/01)**
By the 1950s, tractors were becoming common on County Down farms, and machines such as this portable threshing machine could be powered by a belt attached to a fly-wheel on the tractor. The tractor could also power a baler, as here. These photographs were taken by D J McNeill on the Flynn farm at Dromara, around 1960.

**Fig 24 Sheep shearing (05/35/33)**
This photograph was taken at John Martin's farm in Drumaghlis, in 1937. Mr Martin is clipping the sheep, helped by Mrs Emily Moss. The woman holding the child is Mrs Margaret Neill. The child is Margaret Neill, later Mrs Hamilton.

**Fig 25 Agriculture class farm visit (DJ48/02/661/02)**
An Agricultural School was established in Downpatrick in 1903. In the 1950s, the agriculture course at Downpatrick Technical College continued this work, combining study, practical work and farm visits, as here at McMillen's farm in Crossgar in 1957. The pig in the photograph is a Large White York, the breed that replaced the Large White Ulster, and now the most common breed of pig in the world. This visit was photographed by D J McNeill.

**Fig 26 A Cow on the railway track (DJ48/01/28/01)**
The railway track shown here was at Ferryhill, Dundrum, part of the Belfast and County Down Railway system. Around 1952, when the photograph was taken by D J McNeill, the most common cattle in County Down were Shorthorns.

**Fig 27 Swimming cattle (05/63/43)**
These cattle are being brought to Taggart Island in Strangford Lough. Even the small islands in the lough were used for seasonal grazing. Taggart Island was big enough to have several fully operational farms.

**Fig 28 Cattle on a boat (DJ05/82/53/01)**
Moving livestock around and across Strangford Lough was often easiest done by boat. These cattle are being loaded at Portaferry pier, probably to move them across to Strangford. The export of cattle from County Down to South West Scotland has also been ongoing for hundreds of years. This is a very rare image so, despite it's poor quality, has been included here.

**Fig 29 Milking parlour (DJ48/02/119/14)**

Mechanical milking apparatus was used on some Ulster farms in the 1920s, but specialisation of production and the rapid spread of electricity after the 1940s meant that parlours became much more common. This photograph was taken by D J McNeill during a farm visit by an agriculture class from Downpatrick Technical College.

**Fig 30 Saintfield cattle market (05/86/56)**
Shopkeepers and publicans often saw fair day as a payday, especially if the event was held monthly. Livestock fairs were men's and boy's events, the latter often being kept away from school so that they could help manage the livestock, and learn how to deal. This photograph was taken in 1936.

Fig 31 Lorry with bull's head attached (DJ05/62/37/02)

The establishment of livestock marts led to the rapid decline of regular fairs. This lorry, photographed by D J McNeill near Tyrella around 1982, is decorated with the mounted head of a Highland bull. The lorry probably belonged to the Fitzpatricks of Mountpanther and the driver has been identified as Russell Prescott. The head may be that of 'Rob Roy', which is now a specimen in the Ulster Folk and Transport Museum.

**Fig 32 Old Sheep Market, Downpatrick (DJ05/41/467/01)**
Markets were held more frequently than fairs, but by the early twentieth century, they could be equally specialised. This photograph, copied from an old print by D J McNeill, shows the Sheep Market on Old Circular Road (now St Patrick's Avenue).

**Fig 33 Queue for sheep sales, Downpatrick (DJ05/41/353/13)**
This photograph by D J McNeill shows a section of the mile-long queue for the sheep sales on the Ballydugan Road, in July 1981.

**Fig 34 Sheep mart (DJ05/41/379/03)**
This photograph was taken by D J McNeill on 3rd April 1980, at the sheep mart in Market Street Downpatrick. The auctioneer was Davy Crossan.

**Fig 35 Loading potatoes on a boat at Kilkeel (05/60/27)**
The export of potatoes to Scotland and England was established by the early twentieth century. In the 1950s, potatoes accounted for 75% of the value of crop exports from Northern Ireland. However, after the Second World War, potato cultivation declined sharply in the county.

Acreage of Potatoes in County Down
1945 - 42,674 acres
1959 - 19,262 acres.

# CHAPTER 3

## Thoughts on a museum collection

Brian S Turner

I saw the man jump out of the group and grasp the handles of the plough. He steadied himself and began to address his companions. He lifted one hand and pointed ahead. He named the parts. He spoke of horses and ploughing points. He strained and balanced and explained. Against the grey stone wall of the old gaol yard he conjured up the green fields of another life.

One of the nurses who came with the visiting party said to me: "Do you know, that's the first time he has spoken for three years."

Few people get the opportunity to establish a museum. When I was given this task in Downpatrick in 1981 I was already very clear that while museums were about objects, those objects had no significance without people. People make things for particular purposes; they use them, they value them, they discard them, they contemplate them. Museums try to understand objects in order to reach the people behind them, and so we add to the meaning of our own lives.

It is important for all kinds of museums to remind themselves, and everybody else, that their collections and their jobs are only validated by people and their ongoing stories. And regional museums, like Down County Museum, must not aspire to be small versions of national museums, but to fill the unique role, given to them by geography, of exploring the particular stories of their communities. This is not to be confused with provincialism, but entails the much more liberating and universal notions which can emerge from a confident, curious, and outward looking parochialism. The 'provincial' mind has one point of nervous reference, that which ties it to the metropolis, while, on the other hand, my parish can talk to your parish through a web of connections which roams freely through all human experience.

So what themes could a small museum established in eighteenth century gaol buildings in Downpatrick call its own? It seemed logically straightforward. We were in a gaol, so gaols and crime and punishment were an obvious subject; and transportation of convicts to Australia provided the international dimension. We were in Downpatrick, so St Patrick and Early Christianity in Ireland gave us connections throughout Ireland and the world. The Vikings who arrived in Ireland in the late eighth century, and named Strangford Lough, allowed us to build triangular connections with both Norway, whence they originated, and Normandy, from where their French speaking descendants also came to Ireland.[1]

So what of farming? In the 1980s it seemed particularly urgent to collect objects which related to our area's main industry and dominant way of life in the horse drawn era, before the local examples and memories had entirely died away. Old farm machinery has a particularly evocative attraction, demonstrated not only in museum collections but in the painted ploughs and turnip cutters which adorn front gardens, as if we have a deep need to hang on to some elements of the life we think they represent. Ulster farm carts might have had a higher survival rate if so many of them were not invited to rot away as brightly presented flower containers at the entrances to so many of our towns and villages.

Collecting old farm machinery might seem like a very obvious, and rather clichéd, activity for a rural museum. In County Down, the birthplace of Harry Ferguson, it was bound to be a concern. His invention of the three-point linkage, enabling implements to be mounted on a light tractor rather than being towed, can be argued to have marked the end, for the moment, of horse-drawn agriculture. Although the Ulster Folk and Transport Museum, with its national collections, is sited in the extreme north of the county, no other museum service in County Down has made such a collection.

In the 1980s Northern Ireland was continuously in the news because of violent social disruption and repeated tragedy. On the other hand the long queues of farmers with their animal trailers waiting to enter Downpatrick mart testified to the ongoing necessities of ordinary life in County Down (see Fig 33 in Chapter 2). In the museum, it was important to show that our collections were relevant to the evolution of everyday life, and not simply as playthings of the intellectually elevated. And so, despite the fact that we began among the ruins of an eighteenth century gaol, and that our first ten years were dominated by finding money to restore the windows, floors, and roofs over our heads, (not to mention clearing up bomb damage to part of the building and frequent security call-outs), the agriculture collection began. It was not an esoteric exercise, but a direct method of communicating with our audience, our support, and our community.

Beginning a collection in such circumstances, in a ruined building and with many other calls on staff time, necessitated compromises with which many museums with limited resources will be familiar. There is a difference between collection and curation, of which staff were fully aware. However there was a strong feeling that material had to be collected or lost, and that detailed interpretation must wait for less hectic times. On the other hand the process of raising awareness of the museum, and the activity of committed staff, encouraged community support, and many gifts to the collections. Through personal contacts, and talks to organisations like Women's Institutes and historical societies, we indicated the areas and objects we were interested in. Gifts came

Fig 1 Douglas Hurd MP, then Secretary of State for Northern Ireland, and Cecil Maxwell, then Chairman of Down District Council, look at part of the farming collection in the museum yard, April 1985. (DCM50/04/04) Photograph by Robin Carter.

Fig 2 Thomas Cromie with a farm cart outside the old gaol, August 1982. Note the refuse skip and the sign on the derelict building, 'To be restored for Down Museum'. (DCM50/01/17) Photograph by Brian S Turner.

from all over the place, objects large and small, together with information and support which was valued and long-lasting. The objects to do with farming were just one aspect of the growing collection, but they were especially useful in linking the museum with its particular hinterland. And despite the physical conditions in which we were operating, there was a growing obligation to make the gifts visible (Fig 1).

People come to mind. Frank Maxwell of Ballee had been part of the group campaigning for a museum for Down since the 1960s. The Maxwell family horse-racing stables, established after his retirement from the linen industry, made for an untypical farm, and Frank was an untypical man, widely read with immense but modestly carried knowledge of local history in Lecale. The late Thomas Cromie who farmed at Grallagh, Rathfriland, arrived

Fig 3 William and Samuel Nesbitt of the Woodgrange, Downpatrick, with their early twentieth-century reaper and binder, en route to the museum, October 1982. (DCM50/01/19) Photograph by Brian S Turner.

Fig 4 William Francis Jackson of Barnamaghery with the Henry Cargo plough, January 1983. (DCM50/02/02) Photograph by Brian S Turner.

on the scene full of enthusiasm (Fig 2), and towing his trailer with donations not only from himself but from his neighbours. John McGiffert of Rathcunningham, Killyleagh, provided much information, gifts and, on occasion, a large van to transport specimens and equipment. Willie and Sam Nesbitt of the Woodgrange, Downpatrick, helped our publicity by being photographed pulling their early twentieth century McCormick reaper and binder, thought to be the first in east Down, through the streets to the museum (Fig 3). The late W F Jackson, whose extended family have farmed in Barnamaghery, near Saintfield, for many generations, provided me with one of life's landmarks (Fig 4). He couldn't walk very well when I knew him, but that did not stop him driving at speed around County Down in his small red car, often stopping outside the museum, blowing the horn until somebody came out. In my journeys around mid-Down with him he displayed knowledge of his place and a way of life in the horse-drawn age which deserved more attention than it was possible to give. His method could be direct. We could drive into a farmyard and he would lower the car window and speak to the first person who approached, "This is Dr Turner. He's from the museum. I'm sure you have stuff here you could give him." This approach would leave me struggling with my idea of social niceties and the theories of museum collecting policy, but was often extremely effective, not only in adding to the collection, but in demonstrating the helpful good nature and genuine interest of the many County Down people we encountered.

Two major donations in the 1980s greatly increased the potential of the collection. Mr and Mrs Samuel Clements of Annacloy presented much of the machinery and tools used by Mrs Clement's father, the late Edward Rea of Annacloy. Mr Rea had farmed entirely in the horse drawn era and, because he was not directly succeeded by a more mechanised farmer, his equipment gained historical value from the fact that it remained much as he had left it (Fig 5). Hugh and Alfie Linehan of Ardmeen gave us the remaining contents of the farmyard of the brothers Patrick and James Denvir of Ballybeg who were locally regarded as good farmers who, while well-versed in old ways, were also prepared to innovate in their younger days (Fig 6). They had, for example, one of the first Ferguson tractors to be used in County Down. Twenty years later Alfie Linehan increased the significance of this gift by presenting a collection of documents relating to the same farm.

Most of our donations came from what would now be seen as comparatively small family farms with the typically mixed arable and livestock economy which prevailed in most of County Down until the second half of the twentieth century. Subsequently, as farming became more mechanised and specialised, locally made implements and tools became completely superfluous,

Fig 5 The late Hugh Hampton unloading a cart from Annacloy, September 1983. (DCM50/02/09) Photograph by Brian S Turner.

Fig 6 Denvir's stackyard, Ballybeg, photographed by D J McNeill, 1955. Left to right are James Denvir, Patrick Denvir, John Telford and Alan Freeman. (DCM05/03/69/01)

and even mass-produced objects which had been commonplace became rare and misunderstood, even by the children and grandchildren of those who had the skills to use them. Nevertheless these objects retain a particular power to interest people and we were helped by young and old to pass on some knowledge of previous ways of life and modes of thought (Fig 7).

Patsy Mullen, a gifted country engineer, was one of those who realised that local action should be taken. Over many years he had made an extensive collection of his own to document the history of his town and district of Castlewellan (Fig 8). In the 1990s he decided that it needed the assurance of a more permanent home. His gift to Down County Museum consisted of many hundreds of objects, not only relating to agriculture but to all aspects of social history which became available to him. Patsy Mullen's standards of care for his collection, his encouragement of historical interest among others within his community, and his deliberate sharing of his collection with children and adults for many years, emphasises the high degree of responsibility which museums and their governing bodies, in this case, Down District Council, take on when they agree to care for the life's work of such a person. It is a trust to be taken very seriously.[2]

Fig 7 Members of Saul Youth Club, help to clean a tumble churn, 1984. From left: Tim Bonnar, Kerry Smyth, Brenda Hampton, and Paula Holland. (DCM50/03/20) Photograph by Robin Carter.

Farmers and farming families are guardians of an intimate knowledge of their own particular piece of our

Fig 8 Patsy Mullen amongst his collection, Castlewellan, 1997. (DCM50/30)

environment. The late Minnis Auld and his brothers, George and David (Fig 9), who farmed their respective drumlins in the adjacent Presbyterian townlands of Ballymacashen, Balloo, and Ballymacreely, just inland from Killinchy, provided an interesting connection between the soil and academia, when they were informants for Professor Robert Gregg of the University of British Columbia in his pioneering work in the 1950s and 60s to define the elements and boundaries of Ulster Scots speech. Minnis Auld could discourse on many subjects, from the building and preservation of traditional Ulster gateposts to, like other donors such as the Hendersons of Clay near Killyleagh, the Presbyterian Home Rulers of east Down in the late nineteenth and early twentieth centuries. I seem also to remember Mrs Auld's kitchen, and home-made bread and blackcurrant jam. Behind each gift to a museum are people and stories which a wise society will provide the resources to understand and to value.

The museum did its best with limited resources and amidst the turmoil of a major building restoration. Agricultural implements were almost the only objects from the collection which could be exhibited in the gaol yard during the ten years of its initial development. They attracted a varied audience and helped to stimulate interest in all kinds of other subjects. Public conservation of implements in the yard, especially when they were accompanied by the authoritative and

Fig 9 George and Minnis Auld, Balloo, Killinchy, 1986. Whereas some farmers demolish traditional Ulster gateposts to make way for larger machinery, the Auld brothers jacked up the right hand pillar in this photograph and moved it over to widen the gateway. Photograph by Brian S Turner. (DCM05/61/40)

engaging explanations provided by the late Brian Magee of Strangford, who worked on the collection in the mid 1980s, effectively illustrated the intention of our community museum (Fig 10).

The opening paragraph of this short note demonstrates, I hope, that objects have a power beyond themselves, and also that museums may have power that is not always recognised or effectively channelled. This power can appear even in incongruous situations, such as the sight of agricultural implements in a gaol yard. But it is better if the surroundings can be more appropriate. Some time after Down District Council acquired the Delamont estate, near Killyleagh, in 1985, the museum proposed a scheme under which its agricultural collection might transfer to the buildings of the Delamont Model Farm which stood derelict at the centre of the estate. These buildings, dating from the 1840s, are an almost intact survival from a period of 'agricultural enlightenment' and improvement which not only marked a major transition in farming practice, but also remind us that east Down played a significant role in the process. The Killyleagh, Killinchy, Kilmood and Tullynakill Farming Society, founded in 1818, and one of whose prize medals is in the museum collection, was one of the oldest such improving societies in Ulster (see Fig 4 in Chapter 5). In this context the preservation of the Delamont farm buildings has the potential to reflect as much credit on those concerned

Fig 10 Brian Magee considers how to tackle the restoration of a hay-kicker, 1985. Photograph by Robin Carter. (DCM50/04/01)

as had the restoration of the only surviving eighteenth century Irish County gaol to serve as the headquarters of Down County Museum. Unfortunately the farm buildings were not acquired by the Council with the rest of the estate and protracted negotiations did not succeed in reaching a situation where the obvious linkage between the museum collection and the important architecture of the historic farm could be used to provide a centrepiece for Delamont Park. Today, the farm buildings are still, sadly, derelict, yet another example of the many buildings at risk in our countryside (Fig 11).

Fig 11 The model farm buildings at Delamont, photographed in 2009.

Despite the apparently conventional collection of obsolete agricultural implements in a rural area I hope it has been shown that, as well as the intrinsic significance of the objects themselves, the collection can also be important in one of the first duties of a regional or local museum. That is to introduce, or re-introduce, the community to itself. Part of that introduction is to our own environment, and the factors that are imposed on us by where we live. City folk may think of all farms and farmers as being the same, but a moment's thought will tell us that stock farming is different from arable farming, and that different skills and equipment are needed by sheep farmers in the Mournes from those required in the grain lands of Lecale or among the vegetable growers of north Down. The small mixed farm of family memory was almost swept away by the enormous changes in agriculture in the half century after the Second World War. Yields of all kinds went up, while the required manpower went down. Vast buildings and enormous machines have imposed themselves on the landscape (Fig 12), and standards of living have changed almost beyond recognition. In this context bygone objects can give us pause for thought about social as well as industrial change, and strike a chord in much of the museum's potential audience, providing a channel by which knowledge and communication can flow in and around all sorts of subjects which may not, at first sight, seem to be related.

Fig 12 Late twentieth century farming changed the landscape – Lord Dunleath's silo on the Vianstown Road. Photographed by D J McNeill, winter 1984. (DCM DJ 05/41/838/05)

Within the museum collection there may also be objects of more than ordinary significance in themselves. In 1980, for example, it was thought possible that the east Ulster 'trottle car' might be extinct and that it would be impossible to find examples to study. The trottle car, known in some areas as a 'truckle car', is a descendant of the Irish 'low backed car', a term made familiar by the mid-nineteenth century song written by the poet and novelist Samuel Lover, and popularised in early sound recordings by Count John McCormack.

*When first I saw sweet Peggy,*
*'Twas on a market day,*
*A low-back'd car she drove,*
*And sat upon a truss of hay;*
*But when that hay was blooming grass,*
*And deck'd with flowers of Spring,*
*No flow'r was there that could compare*
*With the blooming girl I sing!*
*As she sat in her low-backed car -*
*The man at the turnpike bar*
*Never asked for the toll,*
*But just rubbed his owld poll*
*And looked after the low-backed car.*

The Irish cart evolved from a platform placed between two parallel poles which were trailed along the ground by a pony, similar to a North-American Indian *travois*. This 'slide car' is an effective means of transport over rough ground and survived into the twentieth century in parts of Ulster. When the poles were raised on two wheels they became more recognisable as the shafts of a cart or 'car'. At first the wheels were solid (Figs 13 and 14), on a revolving axle, and subsequent development of wheel hubs, fixed axles, and spoked wheels resulted in the trottle car, a cart with small wheels and shafts which sloped low to the rear, requiring the body of the cart to be raised at the back to give a level platform (Fig 15).[3] It was only with the introduction of the farm cart with large

Fig 13 Nineteenth century engraving showing a block wheel car at Down Cathedral. (DCM 1984-37)

Fig 14 Block-wheeled car photographed in Glenshesk, north Antrim, by R J Welch (1859-1936), circa 1900. (National Museums Northern Ireland, W01-56-27).

Fig 15 R J Welch photographed this spoke-wheeled trottle car in Islandmagee, County Antrim. No historic photographs of County Down trottle cars in use have yet come to light. (National Museums Northern Ireland, W01-60-11).

wheels, the Scots cart, that the shafts became more or less horizontal when harnessed to the horse, and it was consequently unnecessary to level up the body of the cart at the back.[4] Before the introduction of the Scots carts the wheel cars, probably in various stages of evolution, were very numerous in County Down, being used for moving all kinds of burdens from place to place. For example, in an enumeration of the agricultural resources of twenty townlands around Ardkeen in the south Ards in 1804, there were no large-wheeled 'wagons or carts' but the twenty townlands between them could provide 287 'cars'. Such a statistic helps us to imagine some of the circumstances of a horse-powered economy. (Think of the physical labour involved in moving produce, looking after countless horses, and recycling dung.)

Such locally made wooden vehicles were very vulnerable to casual destruction and, although they do appear in the work of late nineteenth and early twentieth century photographers such as Robert Welch (Figs 14 and 15), very few examples, even of the later spoke-wheeled versions, have survived to be taken into museum collections. Fortunately, my knowledgeable and persistent friend, W F Jackson, managed to locate several trottle cars in mid Down, of which three, somewhat the worse for wear, were taken into the collection.[5] They had survived a bit like horse-powered wheelbarrows, doing humble and almost unseen tasks about the farm, such as carrying dung to the fields for fertilizer (Fig 16). As Wilbur Douglas of Ballykine told us, "The trottle cars were never off the farm, but the big carts were kept good for going into town."

One of the necessary tasks of the local historian, and the local museum, is to distinguish between those elements which were widely distributed and common to many different places, and those which have a particular local significance. Thus, contrasting with mass-produced agricultural implements, the survival of locally made vehicles with a long evolutionary history, such as the

Fig 16 Trottle car in the museum collection, (DB150 DCM1988-10).

trottle cars, provide opportunities for further study by those interested in the history of transport, agriculture, and County Down.

All museum collections can lead our thoughts in different directions. Who were the people who made all these implements. Some worked in large factories, such as Pierce's of Wexford, or McCormick's of Chicago; others may have been the local blacksmiths who both made and repaired the equipment which made farming possible. A look at the jobs mentioned in a blacksmith's account book can give another picture of the necessities of daily life: "cutting a chill plough; one set of horse shoes; sharping the harrowpins; hanging a scythe; steeling a sock; laying the grubber; two new shoes, two removes, one toed; mending a drag; strapping a billhook; making a eye for a gate; splicing a cart shaft."[6] By such minutiae, and such skill, do we survive to live in the present day. So the documentary record is also relevant, and the museum has an archive of documents and photographs which accompanies and elaborates on its three dimensional collections. Much material of this kind still cries out for analysis. Here also are items such as the medals presented by the farming societies of the mid-nineteenth century for such achievements as 'greatest quantity of thorough draining', 'best cultivated root crop', or 'best bull'. These objects are solid evidence to remind us of the concerted efforts at agricultural improvement which were taking place at that time, as, for a different era, do the trophies of the Ardglass Young Farmers Club, in existence from 1932 until 1954, which have been entrusted to the care of the museum. (See Fig 9 in Chapter 4).

In an era when we have become accustomed to the commodification of everything, there is a danger that we forget the human stories, emotions, memories and responsibilities with which museums have been entrusted. This is a great danger, especially as time passes and distance grows between the giver of the gift and the current custodian. I need not mention his name, but I well remember the man from the County Down countryside who came to give one of his most precious possessions to the museum. It was his mother's watch, given to her as a teenager, and carefully kept by her son until near the end of his own long life. "I have nobody to give it to", he said, "so I wonder if the museum would keep it." This illustrates another danger: there is no automatic obligation to take on such a trust, and it would be folly to do so on any basis other than a careful and objective collecting policy. But once it does decide to take such a long-term responsibility, it is a very strong duty, and privilege, for the museum and its governing authorities to fulfil it for public benefit.

## NOTES AND REFERENCES

1. For further elaboration of this strategy in relation to the establishment of Down County Museum see, for example, Brian S Turner, 'Ireland - Division and Diversity', in *Museums in Divided Societies, Proceedings of the Annual Conference of ICOM/ICR 1994*, 20-29. (Ljubljana 1995), and 'Dialogue on Common Ground' keynote address to annual conference of ICOM Norge and Norges Museumsforbund (Norwegian Museums Association), Bergen, 2002.
2. For a discussion of Patsy Mullen's achievement see Linda McKenna, 'The Patsy Mullen Collection' in *Down Survey 1997*, The Yearbook of Down County Museum.
3. G B Thompson, *Primitive land transport of Ulster* (Belfast Museum and Art Gallery monograph, 1958), suggests that the spoke wheeled trottle car may have developed after the introduction of the Scots cart in the late eighteenth century, as an attempt to combine the qualities of the solid wheeled car and the larger cart.
4. Thompson, *op cit*; E Estyn Evans, *Irish Folk Ways*, 165-180 (London 1957).
5. George Thompson, *op cit*, in his careful examination of this subject in the mid-twentieth century, said that he had never seen a trottle car 'or any comparable vehicle' outside County Antrim.
6. Author's notes; extracted from the workbook of James Smyth (d circa 1895) and his son William John Smyth, of Tullintanvally in the parish of Annaclone, County Down, in family possession.

# CHAPTER 4

## Catalogue of Objects

M Lesley Simpson with contributions from all authors

The catalogue lists first those objects relating to arable, then pastoral farming. The largest section deals with crop production and has been arranged so as to follow the farming year. In addition to the large pieces of machinery and smaller hand tools, the museum has relevant archive material of which only a sample is noted here. This would repay much more extensive study. While some objects used in the dairy have been listed, those which would have been in general use, rather than specifically on farms, are not included. Other related objects, such as blacksmithing and veterinary tools are not included.

### CROPS

### Preparing the ground

Three main types of plough were in use in County Down, of which two are represented in the museum collection – wheel ploughs for initial preparation and turning furrows on large, lowland fields and drill ploughs for making raised drills for planting.

#### Ploughs

1. Wheel plough, with swingletree. Bears maker's name 'Howard LBT' and 'Howard England LBT-R'. With knife.
*Given by Mr Stewart Campbell, Grallagh, Rathfriland.*
DB 33 DCM 1984-1

John and Frederick Howard of Bedford established their factory for agricultural implements in 1813. It became one of the largest manufacturers of horse-drawn machinery in England until well into the twentieth century. Horse-drawn wheel ploughs were common on lowland farms in County Down during the first half of the twentieth century.

2. Wheel plough, bearing maker's name 'H Cargo' (see Fig 4 in Chapter 3).
*Given by Mr W F Jackson, Barnamaghery, Crossgar.*
DB 54 DCM 1984-2

This plough was assembled by blacksmith Henry Cargo, of the Inch, Downpatrick, from parts obtained from a local foundry (see invoice, Fig 14). He would have forged coulters and possibly shares, but the body of the plough would have been made up of parts bought from the foundry, and welded together in the forge. Mouldboards had to be cast in the foundry.

The blacksmith had an important role as an intermediary between the foundry and local farmers. He had to understand the technology of the foundry, and the techniques used by farmers. This meant that he could repair parts of broken ploughs, and also set the plough irons to turn different types of furrow. It was standard practice for blacksmiths to put their names on the implements they made.

The donor, Mr Jackson, told us that 'about fifty years ago' ( ie c1930s) the late Johnny Watson of Drumaghlis won the ploughing match at Listooder with this plough. The plough went from the Watsons to John Craigon of Magherascouse, from whom the donor bought it.

3. Wheel plough, with 'universal body', bearing makers' names 'Howard potato plough DDP-R', 'Manufactured by Ransome Sims & Jefferies Ltd Ipswich,' 'T J McErvel Ltd agents Belfast', 'Howard DD3 left ridging' and 'Howard DD8 right ridging' (latter on mould boards).

*Given by Mr William Connor, Greystone Farm, Tollumgrange, Ardglass.*
DB 70 DCM 1984-3

This plough has been assembled from parts manufactured by Howard of Bedford, and Ransomes of Ipswich. The universal body meant that the plough parts could be changed to perform different functions. By the early twentieth century, foundry-made implements had been so standardised it was possible to replace parts of an implement originally manufactured in one foundry with parts made in another (sometimes even another country). McErvel was a well-known dealer in implements.

4. Wheel plough, bearing maker's name 'IRDGP 3M', 'Ransomes Ipswich England' with plough knife, one mould board.
*Given by Mr and Mrs Samuel Clements, Annacloy, Downpatrick.*
DB 68 DCM 1984-8

This is a good example of a standard wheel plough that might have been used on County Down farms as late as 1960, and can still be seen at horse ploughing competitions in the county. Fig 5 in Chapter 1 shows the plough in use.

Fig 1 Oliver Curran, Down District Council, with wooden plough (DB 88 DCM 1988-3).

**5. Wooden plough** (Fig 1).
*Given by Mr Edward and Miss Mary Ellen O'Brien, Dunavil, Kilkeel.*
DB 88 DCM 1988-3

This is a Mourne plough, of fairly recent design. (Ploughs like this were made in Annalong, for example, into the 1960s). One of the original functions of the Mourne plough (turning furrows) has been removed and the plough is made to operate solely as a drill plough. Its asymmetric construction shows its origins, deriving from the common Irish plough of the late eighteenth and early nineteenth centuries.

**6. Drill plough**, bearing maker's name and date 'T Weir 1894'.
*Given by Mr Wilfred Keys, Ballymacarn South, Spa, Ballynhinch.*
DB 116 DCM 1988-5

**7. Drill plough**, bearing maker's name and date 'Weir Ballyroney 1891'.
*Given by Mr R J Cromie, Mount Marble, Grallagh, Rathhfriland.*
DB 313 DCM 1988-52

Weir's foundry at Ballyroney specialised in agricultural equipment, including ploughs, grubbers, barn fans and carts. The foundry was electrified in 1945, and continued production on a small scale until around 1980.

**8. Drill plough**, bearing maker's name and date 'H McCarthy Greyabbey 1887', may include modern parts. With marker (ritter) and chains, hack, drilling tree, two swingle trees and hook. These were used to attach the horses' harness to the plough.
*Given by Mr Hugo McCarthy, Ballycran, Mr Addie Clint, Mr Eamon Woods, Miss Maisie Donnan and Mr Gerald McGrattan, Kircubbin.*
DB 378 and 386 DCM 2008-289/1-6

A blacksmith-made drill plough, used in potato cultivation. Drill plough parts did not require casting, so blacksmiths could manufacture the entire implement, using iron bought from foundries. This plough was made by Hugo McCarthy's grandfather, Hugh McCarthy at his smithy in Greyabbey.

**Harrows**

Four different types of harrow are represented in the collection; the design reflects their function.

1. Saddle harrows, set of two, with adjustable swingletree.
*Given by Mr and Mrs Samuel Clements, Annacloy, Downpatrick.*
DB 69 DCM 1988-12/1-2

2. Saddle harrows, set of two with two swingletrees.
*Given by Mr William and Mr Thomas Girvan, Tullywest, Saintfield.*
DB 85 DCM 1988-15/1-2

Saddle harrows were associated with drill cultivation, used in breaking up soil on ridges The curved 'leaves' meant that the harrow could break up soil and remove weeds from the drills, without flattening them.

3. Pin harrows, set of two.
*Given by Mr and Mrs Samuel Clements, Annacloy, Downpatrick.*
DB 71 DCM 1988-13/1-2

4. Pin harrows set of two, wooden framed.
*Given by Mr R Stevenson, Jericho, Derryboy, Killyleagh.*
DB 183 DCM 1988-17/1-2

5. Pin harrows set of three, bearing maker's name 'T Anderson', a blacksmith, at Toye, near Killyleagh (see invoice, Fig 13).
*Given by Mr John McGiffert, Rathcunningham, Killyleagh.*
DB 343 DCM 2008-290

This type of harrow was used for deepening soil and/or covering seed. The small pins on these implements suggest that they were used for the latter task.

6. Knife harrows, set of three.
*Given by Mr and Mrs Samuel Clements, Annacloy, Downpatrick.*
DB 71 DCM 1988-14/1-3

The large pins on this harrow suggest that it was used to break up soil after it had been ploughed.

7. Spring harrow, bearing maker's name 'Wexford Engineering Co'.
*Given by Mrs Florence McGaffin, Closkelt, Ballyroney, Banbridge.*
DB 168 DCM 1988-16

The curved tines on spring harrows, broke up soil, and collected loose stones. Wexford had several implement making foundries; Wexford Engineering Works was established in the early nineteenth century.

**Field Rollers**
Rollers were used for breaking up the soil after ploughing, for compressing after sowing and for rolling grass.

1. Granite roller.
*Given by Mr William Connor, Tollumgrange, Ardglass.*
DB 70 DCM 1984-9

Stone rollers were favoured for their weight. However, the narrow diameter required for the roller to be operable meant that they tended to sink in soft ground. The construction of the roller in one piece meant that it was difficult to turn at the end of a field and they were also liable to fracture if pulled over uneven stone roads or yards.

2. Roller with wooden frame, one barrel missing.
*Given by Mr Alfie and Mr Hugh Linehan, Ardmeen, Downpatrick.*
DB 139 DCM 1988-18

In 1839, the optimal dimensions for metal rollers were 5-6 feet long, with drums of between 20-30 inches in diameter. These dimensions changed very little. The construction of the drums in two sections made the implement easier to turn.

**Hand tools**
Spades
Turf spades.
1. A slane type turf spade, with the wing on the right hand side of the blade. New blocks of wood have (unusually) been inserted on either side of the shaft.
*Given by the Thompson Brothers, Auctioneers, Downpatrick.*
DB 39 DCM 1984-66

2. A slane type right-footed turf spade, with a horn handle. A new block of wood has been inserted in the foot rest. The blade has been mended.
*Given by Mr Liam Baxter, Rostrevor.*
DB 47 DCM 1984-67

3. A slane type turf spade, with a wing on the left hand side.
*Given by Mr J Bingham, Carnacaville, Newcastle.*
DB 560 DCM 2009-64

4. A slane type right footed turf spade, with a wing on the right hand side.
*Given by Mrs Edith Ash, Killyleagh.*
DB 567 DCM 2009-65

Spade, blade 36 cms long, 12 cms at widest point.
*Given by Mr Pat Brennan, Downpatrick.*
DB 1098 DCM 2008-213

## Sowing and cultivation

**Seed drill**, bearing maker's name 'McCormick International', with wooden wheels.
*Given by Mr Alfie and Mr Hugh Linehan, Ardmeen, Downpatrick.*
DB 139 DCM 1988-35

The horse-drawn seed-drill developed by Jethro Tull in the early eighteenth century, was the most famous invention of the English Agricultural Revolution'. Seed-drills were manufactured in Ireland from the mid-eighteenth century, but they did not become common on County Down farms, where the small acreage of grain grown meant that the seed could easily be sown by hand.

**Turnip Sowers**
Turnip sowers were designed to sow seed evenly along the tops of raised drills. The hour glass shaped roller at the back of the sower compressed the soil in the drill without flattening it.

1. Sower, bearing maker's name 'Philip Pierce & Co. Turnip sower patent no 2'.
*Donor's name withheld.*
DB 76 DCM 1988-29

2. Sower, bearing maker's name 'Pierce Wexford'.
*Given by Mr Edward and Miss Mary Ellen O'Brien, Dunavil, Kilkeel.*
DB 88 DCM 1988-30

Philip Pierce of Wexford's foundry was established in 1837, and became the largest implement manufacturer in Ireland.

3. Sower, bearing maker's name 'Corbett & Williams, Rhuddland New Era', and supplier's name 'Hugh Kelly, Downpatrick'.
*Given by Mr Alfie and Mr Hugh Linehan, Ardmeen, Downpatrick.*
DB 139 DCM 1988-31

Corbett and Williams were implement manufacturers based in Cardiganshire, Wales. Hugh Kelly's store on Market Street, Downpatrick supplied such equipment to local farmers. This sower and other items listed below came from the Denvir farms at Ballybeg (see Chapter 3 for further information and photograph Fig 6, also archive material below). The donors inherited the two Denvir farms.

4. Wooden sower (Fig 2).
*Given by Mr R Stevenson, Jericho, Derryboy, Killyleagh.*
DB 183 DCM 1988-33

This was probably locally made. The sledge runners on each side of the sower meant that it could travel over raised drills without flattening them. The sowing mechanism is similar to that on metal foundry-made sowers.

Fig 2 Wooden sower (DB 183 DCM 1988-33).

**Turnip Thinner**
*Given by Mr Thomas Cochrane, Ballynahinch*
DB 121 DCM 1988-32

**Grubbers and Hoes**
Grubbers were used to weed crops grown in raised drills. The long straight, equidistant rows created by the drills meant that horse-drawn implements could be pulled between the rows of growing plants, without damaging them. The iron toes of the grubber pulled weeds growing along the sides and bottom of the drill.

1. Three-toed grubber.
*Given by Mr and Mrs Samuel Clements, Annacloy, Downpatrick.*
DB 69 DCM 1984-7

2. Three-toed grubber.
*Given by Mr Edward and Miss Mary Ellen O'Brien, Dunavil, Kilkeel.*
DB 88 DCM 1988-22

3. Five-toed grubber, bearing maker's name 'Lowther'.
*Given by Mr W J Henderson, Clea, Killyleagh.*
DB 99 DCM 1988-23

This very large, wheeled grubber (also known as a cultivator) was used for ripping up stubble ground after a grain crop, so that (for example) potatoes could be planted.

4. Five-toed grubber, bearing maker's name 'Hunter Hoe patent Maybole'.
*Given by Mr Alfie and Mr Hugh Linehan, Ardmeen, Downpatrick.*
DB 139 DCM 1988-25

Horse-drawn hoes, like grubbers, pulled weeds out of the sides of raised drills, but they were generally used in the small drills made for growing vegetables other than potatoes or turnips. The 'Hunter Hoe', made at Maybole, Ayrshire, in Scotland was one of the most common horse-drawn hoes used.

5. Five-toed grubber, bearing maker's name 'Star patent' drill hoe.
*Given by Mr Alfie and Mr Hugh Linehan, Ardmeen, Downpatrick.*
DB 139 DCM 1988-26

This grubber was made in the Star Engineering Works in Wexford, one of the four big implement making factories established there in the nineteenth century.

6. Four-toed grubber.
*Given by Mr and Mrs A S Fleming, Coniamstown, Ballynoe, Downpatrick.*
DB 74 DCM 1988-27

This and other items came from the Fleming farm, formerly Hamiltons (Mrs Fleming was a Hamilton). They came to the farm in the early1860s, following the eviction of a family called Starkey.

**Hand tools**

Hoe, described by donor as a 'Shoulder grubber', bearing maker's name 'Monro's Walkover Hoe and Cultivator'.
*Patsy Mullen Collection.*
DB 761 DCM 1997-128

Seed fiddle. 'Perfection' sower, made in Comber, by Jas A Gibson.
*Given by Mr W P Holland, Downpatrick.*
DB 63 DCM 1984-801/2

This was used for sowing seed broadcast.

Seed sower, 'Premier' sower (Fig 3).
*Given by Mr Maurice Patton, Newtownards.*
DB 100 DCM 1986-280

Fig 3 Corn sower (DB 100 DCM 1986-280).

The seed falling from the small sack was flung out by turning a handle rather than using a bow like the one above, which is much more common. The small size of this specimen suggests that it may have been used for sowing flax as well as (or rather than) corn.

Weed pullers

Weed pullers like these were used for pulling individual weeds – especially thistles – out from among growing crops.

Weed pullers, with metal blades and rough (probably home-made) wooden handles.
*Given by Mr and Mrs Eric Gill, Ardglass.*
DB 34 DCM 1984-98

Weed pullers, metal blades, wooden handles.
*Given by Mr and Mrs Samuel Clements, Annacloy, Downpatrick.*
DB 69 DCM 1984-99/1

Wooden weed pullers (Fig 4). This pair was bought at Hugh Dickson's shop in Downpatrick, probably in the 1940s -1950s.
*Given by Mr M Taggart, Lisban, Saul, Downpatrick.*
DB 253 DCM 2009-66

Fig 4 Wooden weed pullers (DB 253 DCM 2009-66).

Two bill hooks and two forked sticks for use with them. These were found in the derelict barn on the late Thomas Kennedy's farm beside Sheepland Windmill, Ardglass.
DB 90 DCM 1985-139/1-2, 1989-16/1-2

These slashers were used to cut back weeds and overgrown hedges. One bears maker's name 'H G Long & Co Sheffield'. The sticks, also known as whin-forks, were used to hold down prickly weeds while they were being cut.

Wooden potato basket.
Wire potato basket.
These were used for carrying seed to drills, or for collecting newly harvested potatoes.
*Given by Mr Wilbur Douglas, Lower Ballykine, Ballynahinch.*
DB 150 DCM 2009-74, 2009-75

Crop sprayer, large wooden barrel with metal spraying mechanism attached.
*Given by Mr Alfie and Mr Hugh Linehan, Ardmeen, Downpatrick.*
DB 140 DCM 2009-68

In 1882, the Bordeaux mix, a combination of copper sulphate and lime, was found to be effective against potato blight (*Phytophthora infestans*). By the early years of the twentieth century, the spraying of potatoes had become almost universal in Ireland. Sprayers attached to the back of a cart could only be used effectively when potatoes were grown in long, straight, equidistant drills.

Animal traps
Two teethed blades snap together when pressure is applied to a metal plate on which bait had been left.

Three animal traps.
*Given by Mr Joseph McAuley, Downpatrick.*
DB 162 DCM 1986-319
*Given by Mr Marshall Magowan, Tullymore, Killinchy.*
DB 222 DCM 1991-91
*Patsy Mullen Collection.*
DB 760 DCM 1997-120

## Harvesting

### Reapers and Mowers

1. Reaper-binder, bearing maker's name 'McCormick Chicago' including replacement shaft (from a reaper). (See Fig 3 in Chapter 3).
*Given by Mr William and Mr Samuel Nesbitt, Woodgrange, Downpatrick.*
DB 43 DCM 1984-4

McCormicks produced the first commercial reaper-binder in 1887. Reaper-binders were labour-saving in that the machine bound grain into sheaves after cutting it. However, they did not become common in Ireland until the First World War, when the government's compulsory tillage policies made it worthwhile for farmers to invest in them.

This machine came to the Nesbitt farm during the First World War. It was bought by John C and W Nesbitt, father and uncle of the donors. The donors thought that it came from a firm called McErvals, for whom the land agent was John Lascelles of Downpatrick. They believe it arrived from Belfast on a train and was driven out to Woodgrange – their aunt remembered meeting it on the road. It was one of the earliest, if not the earliest, in the district.

The reaper and binder was normally drawn by three horses, one extra helping the other two on either side of the shaft. This one was converted, by cutting down the original shaft, for use with a tractor when the Nesbitts bought a Fordson tractor in February 1940. This was one of the first tractors in the district.

2. Reaper, bearing maker's name 'J Wallace & Sons, Glasgow', and two knives.
*Given by Mr and Mrs Samuel Clements, Annacloy, Downpatrick.*
DB 98 DCM 1988-20

**Hay Sweeps, Rakes and Turners**
1. Hay sweep, metal, known as a 'tumbling paddy'.
*Given by Mr William Stevenson, Conlig, Annacloy, Downpatrick.*
DB 56 DCM 1988-41

This is probably an American type of hay sweep, which came into use in the later nineteenth century. As a horse pulled the sweep, it gathered up hay. When the operator judged that enough had been collected, he let the teeth of the sweep lodge lightly in the ground, so that the sweep tumbled over, depositing the heap of hay on the ground. Mr Stevenson remembered this sweep being on the farm for at least fifty years.

2. Hay sweep, metal, bearing maker's name 'Pierce' with tumbling body.
*Given by Mr and Mrs Samuel Clements, Annacloy, Downpatrick.*
DB 69 DCM 1988-42

Manufactured by Pierce of Wexford.

3. Hay sweep, wooden, 'tumbling paddy'.
*Given by Mr Kennedy Bassett, Mullagh, Inch, Downpatrick.*
DB 139 DCM 1988-46

4. Ruck lifter, metal parts only.
*Given by Mr and Mrs Samuel Clements, Annacloy, Downpatrick.*
DB 71 DCM 1988-43

A ruck lifter is a low flat bodied cart, with a winching mechanism at the front. The body of the cart could be tilted so that its back end was lying on the ground. A chain from the winch was put around a ruck of hay and this was then winched up the sloping body of the cart. The winch was usually cast metal, so parts of the ruck lifter had to be made in a foundry.

5. Hay kicker, iron wheeled, doubled forked.
*Given by Mr John Smyth on behalf of the Smyth Family, Tanvalley, Katesbridge.*
DB 78 DCM 1988-45

Horse-drawn hay kickers, or tedders, were developed in Britain in the early nineteenth century. They speeded up the process of turning and spreading hay in windrows.

6. Hay rake, bearing maker's name 'Pierce Victor'.
*Given by Mr Alfie and Mr Hugh Linehan, Ardmeen, Downpatrick.*
DB 139 DCM 1988-47

Horse drawn hay rakes were in common use on larger farms by the later nineteenth century. This artefact, made by Pierce of Wexford, is the most common type. The rake is mounted on a frame set on two wheels. The row of curved teeth at the back collected hay until its own weight caused it to fall over. The slight curve in the teeth meant that the falling bundle of hay fell in a loose roll, which allowed drying air to circulate through its mass.

**Potato Diggers**

1. Digger, bearing maker's name 'Caledonian', with draw bar, spade grips and draw pole.
*Given by Mr and Mrs Samuel Clements, Annacloy, Downpatrick.*
DB 69 DCM 1988-37

The rotary action potato digger was patented by a Mr J Hanson of Doagh, County Antrim in 1855. It became the prototype for similar machines manufactured world wide.

2. Digger, bearing maker's name 'Jack & Sons, Maybole'.
*Donor's name withheld.*
DB 76 DCM 1988-38

Alexander Jack's implement factory at Maybole in Ayrshire functioned between 1852 and 1966. Potato diggers were manufactured by the firm from at least the late nineteenth century.

3. Digger, bearing maker's name 'Martin's Cultivator Co. Ltd Stamford England'.
*Given by Mr W J Henderson, Clea, Killyleagh.*
DB 99 DCM 1988-39

4. Digger, bearing maker's name 'Pollocks Perfect, Ayrshire'. Supplied by T J McErval, Belfast.
Parts broken and missing.
*Given by Mr Gerald Douglas, Bryansford, Newcastle.*
DB 104 DCM 1988-40

**Hand tools**

Scythe, The shaft (or 'sned') is of a Scottish 'y' shape. This was referred to locally as a 'cradle sned'.
*Given by Mr Thomas Seay, Tullinacree, Crossgar.*
DB 59 DCM 1985-200

Modern scythe, bearing maker's name 'Spear and Jackson', with label still attached, apparently unused.
DB 668 DCM 1993-593
Scythe handle. This is a curved 'Yankee' type sned.
DB 668 DCM 1993-594
Scythe blade. DB 668 DCM 1993-595
Reaping hook, smooth-bladed, modern, possibly 1980s.
DB 668 DCM 1993-597
*Given by Mr G Quayle, Belfast.*

The donor used to work for the Department of Agriculture and bought these items at a sale.

Reaping hook, smooth-bladed.
*Patsy Mullen Collection.*
DB 760 DCM 1997-122

Sickle with serrated semi-elliptical serrated blade.
*Anonymous donation.*
DB 362 DCM 2009-69

Two sandstone scythe sharpening stones.
*Patsy Mullen Collection.*
DB 760 DCM 1997-115

These were found on the shore of Castlewellan Lake. They may have belonged to Alfie Gwinn, the fishwarden for the lake during the first half of the twentieth century.

Sharpener for reaper blades (Fig 5).

Fig 5 Sharpener for reaper blades (DB 92 DCM 1985-196).

This has a small sharpening stone at one end, operated by a handle attached to two cog wheels.
*Given by Mr N McCormick, Magherlagan, Downpatrick.*
DB 92 DCM 1985-196

Hand hay rake.
*Given by Mr A Milligan, Edendarriff, Seaforde.*
DB 262 DCM 1988-48
This was known as a 'poor man's rake'. It was bought in Ballynahinch, about 1925-26 at Stewart and Gibsons and had belonged to the Kennedy Family of Drumcaw but never used.

## Storage and processing

**1. Turnip/ potato cutter**, bearing maker's name 'Doyle, Wexford'.
*Purchase.*
DB 38 DCM 1988-49

This, and the following two items, were all used for preparing fodder. Doyle's was one of four major agricultural implement makers established in Wexford in the mid-nineteenth century.

**2. Turnip slicer**, bearing maker's name 'Bentall Unchokable and Chaff Cutter, Bentall'.
*Given by The Auld Brothers, Minnis Auld of Ballymacashen, George Auld of Balloo and David Auld of Ballymacreely, Killinchy.*
DB 145 DCM 1988-53

E H Bentall and Co of Heybridge, began to manufacture turnip cutters in the 1860s, and production continued into the twentieth century. This model may have been driven by a belt attached to a stationary engine.

**3. Turnip slicer**, bearing maker's name 'Philip Pierce'.
*Given by the Smyth Family, Tanvalley, Katesbridge.*
DB 78 DCM 1988-81

Pierce (established in1837) was the largest of the four major agricultural implement makers in Wexford in the mid nineteenth century

**4. Weighbridge** and two 56 lb weights.
*Given by Mr and Mrs Samuel Clements, Annacloy, Downpatrick.*
DB 71 DCM 1988-57/1-3

**5. Corn Grinder**, bearing maker's name 'Wrekin Supreme' made by James Clay, Wrekin Foundry, Ketley, Shropshire.
*Given by Mr McKimm, Boardmills, Lisburn*
DB 84 DCM 1989-15

**6. Wooden barn fan.**
*Given by Mrs P Hanvey, Lisban, Saul, Downpatrick.*
DB 97 DCM 1988-51

Winnowing removes the husks from grain seeds. Before barn fans were invented, winnowing was carried out on a breezy day. The grain was poured from a tray on to a cloth, so that the light husks blew away, while the heavier seed fell on to a cloth. Barn fans were developed in Holland and Scotland during the late eighteenth century. When the handle at the side was turned, the wooden fans set up a current of air, which winnowed grain dropped though the hopper at the top of the machine. By the mid nineteenth century, they were common on most medium sized farms in Ireland.

**Hand tools**
Potato fork or 'shovel'.
*Given by Mr John McRoberts, Rademon, Crossgar.*
DB 59 DCM 1984-100

This was used for lifting potatoes from storage clamps without damaging them.

Hay knives
These were used for cutting blocks of hay from stacks or bales.

Hay knife, bearing maker's name 'Tyzack Sons & Turner Abbeydale Sheffield'.
*Given by Mr and Mrs A S Fleming, Coniamstown, Downpatrick.*
DB 74 DCM 1984-83

Hay knife.
*Given by Mr Maurice Patton, Newtownards.*
DB 99 DCM 1985-151

Three seed testers. Small hollow metal spikes, with a hole at the end, and along one side. They were used to withdraw samples from sacks of grain.
*Patsy Mullen Collection.*
DB 759 DCM 1997-108, DB 760 DCM 1997-119, 121

Rope twisters
1. Rope twister, 'car-crank' type, with a wooden handle, and two pieces of wood on the shaft. Probably locally made.
*Donor's name withheld.*
DB 76 DCM 1984-46

2. Rope twister, 'car-crank' type, with a wooden handle, and three pieces of carefully turned wood on the shaft. It had been used on the donor's farm and was probably also locally made.
*Given by Mr William Kennedy, Dunanelly, Inch, Downaptrick.*
DB 177 DCM 1986-426

3. Rope twister, 'car crank' type, with a wooden handle, and one piece of wood on the shaft.
*Given by Mrs M Jardine, Oughley, Saintfield.*
DB 188 DCM 1986-494

4. Rope twister, 'car-crank' type with a wooden handle, and one piece of wood on the shaft.
*Given by Mr Liam Baxter, Newtown, Rostrevor.*
DB 47 DCM 1984-107/5

5. Rope twister (Fig 6).
This rope twister was constructed to twist three ropes at the same time. The three hooks are fitted to a rectangular wooden frame, on the other side of which is a handle for turning the ropes. It was found on a farm at Ballykinler.
*Anonymous donor.*
DB 136 DCM 1986-397

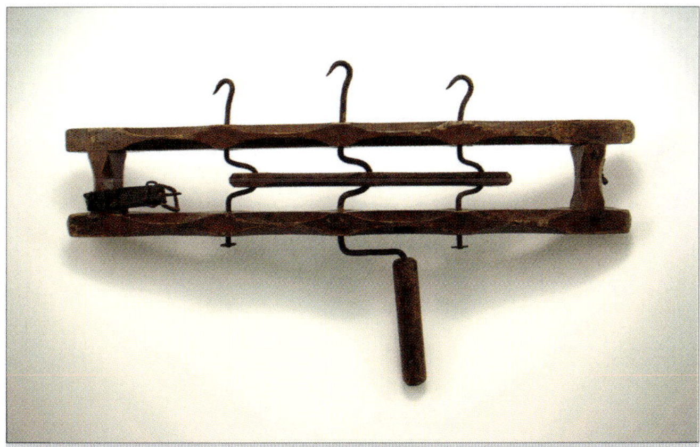

Fig 6 Rope twister (DB 136 DCM 1986-397).

## LIVESTOCK

### Cattle

**Two Bull leaders**. These are hooks operated by chain which runs the length of a wooden pole, about one metre long. The hook is attached to a ring in the bull's nose.
One of these was originally bought in 1920, by Mick Murphy of Leitrim.
*Patsy Mullen Collection.*
DB 760 DCM 1997-113, 114

**Churns**
Plunge churns
Four plunge churns, wooden, stave built, bound with metal hoops.
*Mr Robin Gill, Sheepland More, Ardglass.*
DB 30 DCM 1994-108
*Given by Mr and Mrs H McCartan, Newcastle.*
DB 179 DCM 1986-444
*Given by Mr George Gordon, Dunnanelly, Downpatrick.*
DB 114 DCM 1988-56

*Given by Miss Ellen Hunter, Ballygally, Downpatrick, in memory of her sister Charlotte Elizabeth Hunter.*
DB 557 2009-76

Tumble churns
Tumble churn, bearing maker's name 'Waide and Sons (No 4)'. (See Fig 7 in Chapter 3)
*Given by Mr James A Smyth on behalf of the Smyth Family of Tanvalley, Katesbridge.*
DB 78 DCM 1988-85

Tumble churn.
*Given by Mr and Mrs E Murnin, Magheralone, Ballynahinch.*
DB 282 DCM 1988-67

Horse operated churns
Churn, horse operated, canopy missing.
*Given by Mr Thomas Cochrane, Ballynahinch.*
DB 121 DCM 1988-78

Churn frame, horse operated, decorated metal frame, churn and staff missing, made by William Weir of Ballyroney. Information about the Weir Foundry can be found in the section on ploughs, above.
*Given by Mr and Mrs Elliot, Tirkelly, Ballyroney, Rathfriland.*
DB 121 DCM 1988-79

Other churns
Churn, metal with lid, 67 cms high, 34.5 cms diameter.
*Given by Mr and Mrs S Clements, Annacloy, Downpatrick.*
DB 71 DCM 1998-58

**Small dairying items**
Churn scrubber, bristles bound with string.
*Given by Mr J J McKinney, Douglas, Isle of Man, formerly of Loughinisland.*
DB 360 DCM 2009-70

This originally came from the home of Mrs H Morgan of Edendarriff and was thought by the donor to date to about the 1930s.

Butter pats, six and butter scoop, all wooden
*Given by Mr and Mrs S Clements, Annacloy, Downpatrick.*
DB 68 DCM 1984-76/1-6, 1984-77

Butter pats, two, scoop and stamp with thistle pattern, all wooden.
*Given by Mrs R Henderson, Toye, Killyleagh.*
DB 175 DCM 1986-406/1-2, 1986-407, 1986-408

Butter bowl, wooden, diameter 49.5 cms.
*Given by Mr John Smyth on behalf of the Smyth Family of Tanvalley, Katesbridge.*
DB 78 DCM 1985-126

Butter bowl, wooden, diameter 40 cms.
*Given by Mrs Sarah Brown, Ballymacarn South, Spa, Ballynahinch.*
DB 164 DCM 1986-336

Butter bowl, wooden, diameter 22 cms.
*Given by Mrs J Jardine, Saintfield.*
DB 182 DCM1986-455

Butter bowl, diameter 34 cms.
*Patsy Mullen Collection.*
DB 785 DCM 1997-454

Cream separator, bearing maker's name 'Lister Ball Bearing'.
*Given by Mr John Smyth on behalf of the Smyth Family of Tanvalley, Katesbridge.*
DB 78 DCM 1984-103

Milk measure. This was used by Ministry of Agriculture officials to take milk samples from local farms.
*Patsy Mullen Collection.*
DB 759 DCM 1997-107

Floating Dairy Thermometer, glass in card tube.
*Given by Mrs Elizabeth Baxter, Newtownards.*
DB 975 DCM 2001-47

## Sheep

**Sheep shears**
The blades are joined by a curved piece of flattened metal, which provides the spring to separate the blades.

Two pairs of sheep shears.
*Given by Mr Marshall Magowan, Tullymore, Killinchy.*
DB 221 DCM 1987-204
*Given by the Jackson Family, The Bank, Barnamaghery, Crossgar.*
DB 915 DCM 1999-368

## Horses

**Curry comb**, used for grooming horses.
*Given by Mr Liam Baxter, Rostrevor.*
DB 47 DCM 1985-107/3

**Horse muzzle**, wire, edge bound with leather.
*Given by Mr Samuel Curlett, Sufficial Quarter, Annacloy, Downpatrick.*
DB 113 DCM 1985-145

The donor told us that this muzzle was used on the horse nearest the corn when reaping because 'the horse might sometimes take a dive into the corn to get a mouthful'.

**Two horse bits**, bar bits.
*Given by Mr and Mrs Samuel Clements, Annacloy, Downpatrick.*
DB 71 DCM 1986-499/1- 2

**Horse clipping machine**, bearing maker's name 'Stewart no1 clipper'.
*Patsy Mullen Collection.*
DB 763 DCM 1997-172

**Horse collar**, part of the harness, used for farm work.
*Given by Mr Maurice Patton, Newtownards.*
DB 100 DCM 2009-77

## Pigs

**Two hooks**, metal, for hanging slaughtered pigs. One is a horizontal beam with a hook at either end and a swivel attachment in the centre. The other is made up of two hooks, hanging from a central, vertical, hooked rod.
*Patsy Mullen Collection.*
DB 759 DCM 1997-110, 111

## Poultry

**Egg Incubator**.
*Given by Miss Maire Hanna, Downpatrick.*
DB 97 DCM 1988-80

The egg industry, traditionally controlled by women, has been big business in Ireland for more than a century. Hatching eggs in an incubator was a move towards intensification of poultry production. Many incubators were provided by big poultry firms from the 1930s onwards.

## TRANSPORT AND POWER

**1. Slipe.**
*Given by Mr Thomas Watson, Killinchy Woods, Crossgar.*
DB 592 DCM 2008-182

Slipes were wheel-less vehicles, set on runners. They were used in boggy ground, or when conditions were particularly muddy. They were made in different sizes and had more or less complicated construction. This slipe was probably used to move seed or manure.

It was used on the donor's farm at Killinchy Woods up to the 1940s.

**2. Converted trottle (or truckle) car**, fitted with tractor draw bar and car tyres. With separate horse shafts for the car, not the same age but made for it (Fig 7).
*Given by the Auld Brothers, Minnis Auld of Ballymacashen, George Auld of Balloo and David Auld of Ballymacreely, Killinchy.*
DB 145 DCM 1988-9

The car has a tipping mechanism, operated by releasing a bar at the front of the car body. This mechanism was particularly associated with County Down.

The donors told us that the car came from Davy Dugan of Barnamaghery to John Heron of Ballymacreely. In 1969 the Aulds borrowed it from John Heron and used it with a horse to clear the overgrown lane to George Auld's house. John Heron did not want it back and gave it to them. The original horse shafts were broken around this time and a new set made (as noted above). However, a tractor draw bar was then fitted.

Fig 7 Converted trottle car (DB 145 DCM 1988-9).

**3. Trottle car**, complete although in poor condition (see Fig 16 in Chapter 3).
*Purchase.*
DB 150 DCM 1988-10
The vendor told us that these cars 'were quite a common thing within about two miles of Ballynahinch but were never off the farm. They were used for carting dung out to the fields etc and were hard worked. Around Lisburn people would take the wings off the big carts if they were doing dirty work in the fields and wash down the carts afterwards. The origin of this cart was unknown but the strong likelihood is that it was partly made and assembled on the farm in Ballykine by a joiner from Ballynahinch called John Black and his brother Jimmy, perhaps about 1900. The Blacks customarily worked this way'.

**4. Trottle car**, poor condition. This was used on the Stewart farm.
*Given by Mr Raymond Stewart, Killybawn, Barnamaghery, Crossgar.*
DB 168 DCM 1988-11

**5. Farm cart**, bearing a plate with the name 'James Blain, Burren'. Base restored. The vendor had bought it from the farm where it worked.
*Purchase.*
DB 33 DCM 1984-5

**6. Farm cart**, (see Fig 5 in Chapter 3).
*Given by Mr and Mrs Samuel Clements, Annacloy, Downpatrick*
DB 68 DCM 1984-6
The cart body can be tipped by releasing a bar at the front. This has been claimed to be a feature of many carts in mid Down.

**7. Spring cart or trap.**
*Given by Mr Norman Richey, Hollymount, Downpatrick.*
DB 98 DCM 1988-7

**8. Box trap or jaunting car.** This originally came from Naas, Co Kildare. Poor condition.
*Given by Mr Owen Kerr, Strangford.*
DB 92 DCM 1988-8

**9. Ferguson Tractor** (Fig 8).
*Purchased with money placed in donation boxes by visitors to the museum.*
DB 577 DCM 2006-15

Fig 8 Ferguson tractor, with, left to right, Gerard Lennon, former Education Officer at Down County Museum, Geoff Davidson, Downpatrick Technical College and Jim Milligan, former owner of the tractor (DB577 DCM2006-15).

A 'Wee Grey Fergie', 1950, registration number 320 GXE. This tractor spent most of its working life at the RAF base at Bishopscourt.

## BOUNDARIES

**1. Iron Gate.** (See Fig 1 in Chapter 3)
*Given by Mr Frank J Maxwell, Church Ballee, Downpatrick.*
DB 86 DCM 1989-1

This was specially made to fit between two stone pillars on the donor's land by Hugh Magilton of Ballybrannagh.

Hugh Magilton died in 1876. His son, also Hugh, died in 1907. It is not certain which one made the gate. Both were blacksmiths and gatemakers at Ballybrannagh. Their best gate is said by the family to be one at Ballee Non-Subscribing Presbyterian Church.

**2. Post hole borer**, bearing maker's name 'Hardypick Limited Sheffield England'.
*Given by Mr G Quayle, Belfast.*
DB 668 DCM 1993-596

## TROPHIES AND MEDALS

### Trophies

Nine cups, trophies from the Ardglass Young Farmers' Club (Fig 9).
The club was founded in 1932 and ceased operation in 1954.
1. Cup with lid, EPBM – Britannia metal.
'Ardglass Challenge Cup presented by Ardglass Young Farmers Club for competition at their annual ploughing match 1948.'
DB 142 DCM 1986-7/1
2. Cup, silver.
'Perpetual Challenge Cup presented to Ardglass Young Farmers' Club in memory of Richard Clinton (their first leader) by members of the club and other friends 1938'.
DB 142 DCM 1986-7/2
3. Cup, silver.
'Bishopscourt Cup presented to the Ardglass Young Farmers Club by Messrs Sharvin & Press. 1946'.
DB 142 dcm 1986-7/3

Fig 9 Trophies, Ardglass Young Farmers' Club (DB 142 DCM 1986-7/1-9).

4. Cup with ebony handles, EPNS.
'Presented to Ardglass Young Farmers Club by Downpatrick Co-operative Agricultural Society Ltd 1939.'
DB 142 DCM 1986-7/4
5. Cup, EPNS.
'Presented to Ardglass Young Farmers Club by John Thompson & Sons Ltd Donegall Quay Mills Belfast 1939'.
DB 142 DCM 1986-7/5
**6. Cup, silver.**
'Presented to the Ardglass Young Farmers Club by F. G. Gill. 1946'.
DB 142 DCM 1986-7/6
7. Cup, EPNS.
'Presented by James Elliott & Co Ltd to Ardglass Young Farmers Club'.
DB 142 DCM 1986-7/7
8. Cup, silver.
'Presented to Ardglass Y.F.C. By W.L.Chambers. to encourage the art of public speaking'.
DB 142 DCM 1986-7/8
9. Cup with lid, EPNS.
'Ballylig Challenge Cup presented to Ardglass Young Farmers Club by David Wilson esq. 1949'. EPNS
DB 142 DCM 1986-7/9
*Given by Mr Robin Gill, Sheepland More, Ardglass and Mr William Crea, Ballyculter, Strangford, on behalf of the trustees of the club.*

**Medals**
Nineteenth-century medals are discussed in chapter 5.

Five medals, awarded to Mrs Isobel McClenaghan, Rathfriland (Fig 10).
1. Gold medal.
Obv: The National Utility Poultry Society
Rev: National Test 1929-1930 Section xiii Mrs I McClenaghan 4 Rhode Island Reds 944 eggs score value 944
28mm diam
DB 1080 DCM 2008-194
2. Silver medal.
Obv: The National Utility Poultry Society
Rev: National Test 1929-1930 Section xiii Mrs I McClenaghan 4 Rhode Island Reds 345 eggs first 16 weeks
51mm diam
DB 1080 DCM 2008-195
3. Silver medal.
Obv: Image of horse
Rev: Kilkeel Agricultural Show 1928 Challenge Medal presented by Capt Nugent Ballyedmond Killowen for the best foal yearling or two year old progeny of Sanhedrin
DB 1080 DCM 2008-196
44mm diam
4. Bronze medal.
Obv: The Jersey Cattle Society of Ulster

Fig 10a Medals awarded to Isabel McClenaghan of Rathfriland, obverse (DB 1080 DCM 2004-194 to 198).

Fig 10b Medals awarded to Isabel McClenaghan of Rathfriland, reverse (DB 1080 DCM 2004-194 to 198).

Rev: Awarded to Mrs Isabel McClenaghan for Jersey cow Millicent in the milk and butter fat competition 1927
DB 1080 DCM 2008-197
44mm diam
5. Bronze medal.
Obv: Awarded to Mrs Isabel McClenaghan for Jersey cow Fryland Mary 2nd in the milk and butter fat competition1933
Rev: The Jersey Cattle Society of Ulster
44mm diam
DB 1081 DCM 2008-198
*Purchase.*

Three silver medals, awarded to Gerald Annesley of Castlewellan (Fig 11).
1. Obv: Royal Ulster Agricultural Society
Rev: Annual Show 1956 awarded to Mr G F Annesley to commemorate win of Irish Aberdeen Association Cup for best group of IAA animals
45mm diam
DB 1120 DCM 2007-266
2. Obv: Irish Polled Aberdeen Angus Association founded 1894
Rev: RUAS May 1937 won by Mr G F Annesley for Best Group in Aberdeen Angus
44mm diam
DB 1120 DCM 2007-267

Fig 11 Medals awarded to Gerald Annesley of Castlewellan (DB 1120 DCM 2007-265 to 267).

3. Obv: Irish Polled Aberdeen Angus Association founded 1894
Rev: RUAS Show 1939 won by GF Annesley Fairy of Borgie
44mm diam
DB 1120 DCM 2007-265
*Purchase assisted by the Northern Ireland Museums Council.*

## ARCHIVE MATERIAL

As indicated in the introduction to this catalogue, we have made no attempt to list all relevant items here. What we thought was more important, in the present context, is to provide examples of the kind of material in the archive. There are books, manuals and notebooks; papers relating to rentals and sales of land; catalogues and lists of farming equipment; account books, invoices and receipts; posters and notices; and various items produced by farming organisations such as local societies, government and educational bodies. Full details are available for anyone wishing to do further research.

The following Resolution
was passed at a Meeting of the
Council of the
Chemico Agricultural Society,
held in the City Hall,
on the 8th February, 1895.
That the Committee
have received with
much regret a letter from
Dr Hodges, resigning his
position as Chemist to the

Fig 12 Presentation address to Henry Hodges, 1895 (DB 1170 DCM 2008-370).

**1. Presentation address to Dr Hodges, 1895** from the Council of the Chemico-Agricultural Society, on his resignation as chemist to the Society (Fig 12).
The purchase also included papers by Dr Hodges on Feeding stuffs, Chemistry for bleachers, an Experimental Agricultural Station and 'What science can do for the Irish farmer'. The latter was an introductory lecture on agricultural chemistry delivered before the members of the Seaforde and Hollymount Farming Society in 1844. This was the first dissertation on soil science in Ireland.

*Purchase, assisted by the Northern Ireland Museums Council.*
DB 1170 DCM 2008-370

Dr John Frederick Hodges was born in Downpatrick in 1815 and died in 1899. He was Professor of Agricultural Chemistry and lecturer on Medical Jurisprudence at Queen's College (later University), Belfast for fifty years. During that time he was Chemical Director of the Chemico-Agricultural Society of Ulster and Editor of the Society's Journal. He founded a Mechanics Institute in Downpatrick, one of the first in Ireland.

His work was recognised throughout Europe, with degrees and honours conferred on him by colleges and societies in Russia, Sweden, Germany, France, Italy and the Netherlands. He was one of the founders of the Royal College of Chemistry, London, President of the Natural History and Philosophical Society of Belfast and twice a Vice-President of the British Association.

**2. Invoice for work done by Thomas Anderson, blacksmith, of the Toye, Killyleagh, 1906-1907**
(Fig 13).
Thomas Anderson made the harrows listed above.
*Given by Mr John McRobert, Rademon, Crossgar.*
DB 71 DCM 1987-51

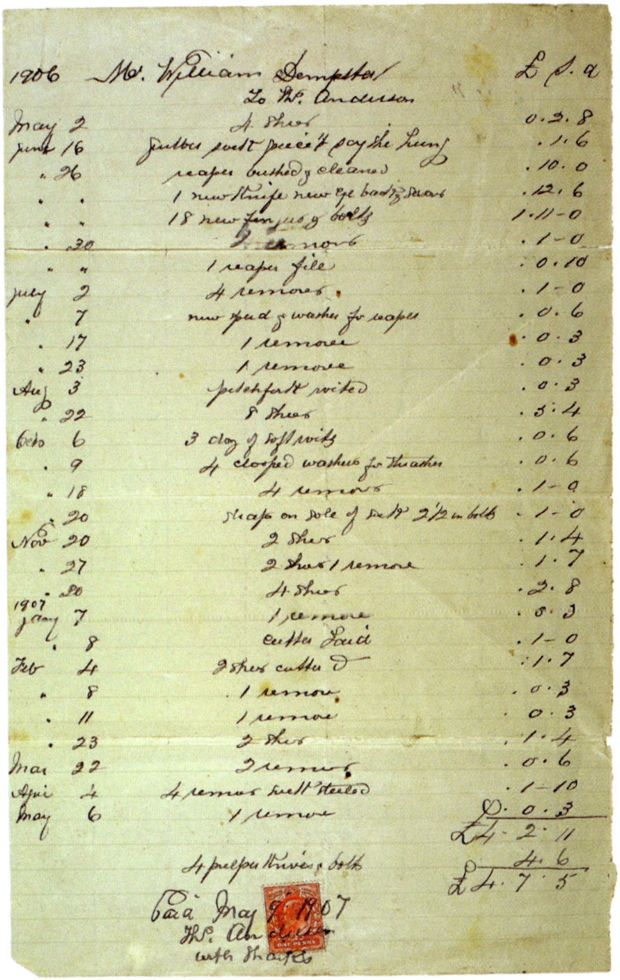

1906 Mr. William Dempster
To Thos Anderson

| | | | £ s. d |
|---|---|---|---|
| May | 2 | 4 shoes | 0.2.8 |
| June | 16 | [illegible] | .1.6 |
| . | 26 | reaper [illegible] cleaned | .10.0 |
| . | . | 1 new knife new eye [illegible] | .12.6 |
| . | . | 18 new fingers & bolts | 1.11-0 |
| . | 30 | [illegible] | .1-0 |
| " | " | 1 reaper file | .0.10 |
| July | 2 | 4 removes | .1-0 |
| . | 7 | new [illegible] washer for reaper | .0.6 |
| . | 17 | 1 remove | .0.3 |
| . | 23 | 1 remove | .0.3 |
| Aug | 3 | pitchfork [illegible] | .0.3 |
| . | 22 | 8 shoes | .5.4 |
| Octo | 6 | 3 [illegible] | .0.6 |
| . | 9 | 4 [illegible] washers for thrasher | .0.6 |
| . | 18 | 4 removes | .1-0 |
| . | 20 | [illegible] | .1-0 |
| Nov | 20 | 2 shoes | .1.4 |
| . | 27 | 2 shoes 1 remove | .1.7 |
| . | 30 | 4 shoes | .2.8 |
| 1907 Jany | 7 | 1 remove | .0.3 |
| . | 8 | cutter laid | .1-0 |
| Feb | 4 | 2 shoes cutter [illegible] | .1.7 |
| . | 8 | 1 remove | .0.3 |
| . | 11 | 1 remove | .0.3 |
| . | 23 | 2 shoes | .1.4 |
| Mar | 22 | 2 removes | .0.6 |
| April | 4 | 4 removes [illegible] steeled | .1-10 |
| May | 6 | 1 remove | 0.0.3 |
| | | | £4.2.11 |
| | | 4 pulper knives & bolts | 4.6 |
| | | | £4.7.5 |

Paid May [illegible] 1907
Thos Anderson
with thanks

Fig 13 Invoice, Thomas Anderson of Killyleagh, 1906-1907 (DB 71 DCM 1987-51).

**3. Invoice for work done by Henry Cargo of the Inch, Downpatrick, 1908-1909** (Fig 14).
This is from a large collection of invoices which came from the Jennings Family of Ballincraig, Inch, Downpatrick. Henry Cargo made the plough listed above. Other invoices in this donation include ones relating to the Downpatrick weighbridge (for weighing cattle and sheep) and the Killyleagh agricultural co-operative society. They date mostly from about 1900-1930.
*Given by Miss Jean Jennings, Ballincraig, Inch, Downpatrick.*
DB 111 DCM 1990-9/1

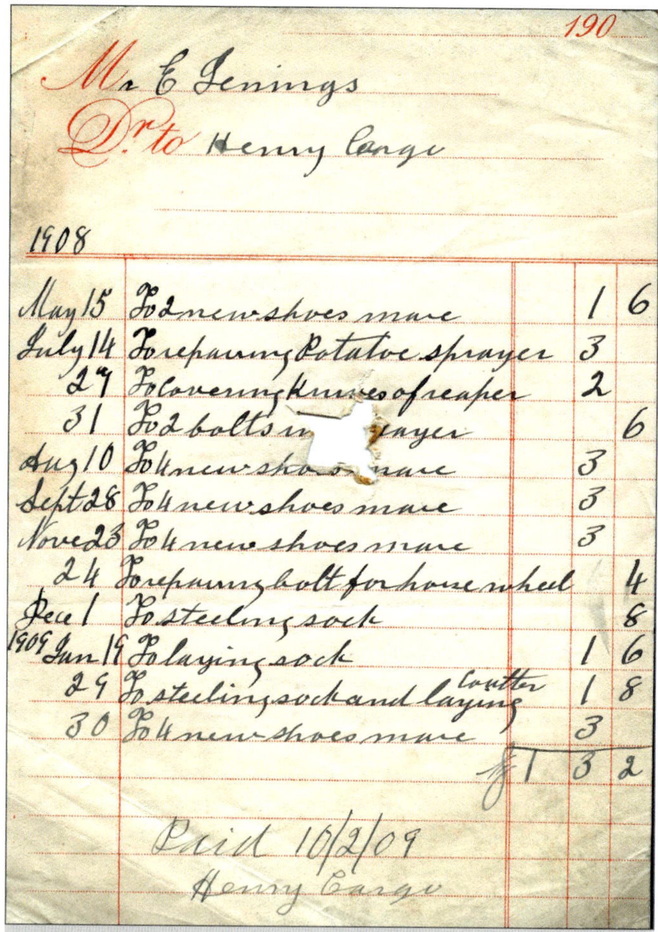

190

Mr E Jennings
Dr. to Henry Cargo

| 1908 | | | |
|---|---|---|---|
| May 15 | To 2 new shoes mare | 1 | 6 |
| July 14 | To repairing Potatoe sprayer | 3 | |
| 27 | To covering knives of reaper | 2 | |
| 31 | To 2 bolts i[illegible]ayer | | 6 |
| Aug 10 | To 4 new sho[illegible] mare | 3 | |
| Sept 28 | To 4 new shoes mare | 3 | |
| Nove 23 | To 4 new shoes mare | 3 | |
| 24 | To repairing bolt for horse wheel | | 4 |
| Dece 1 | To steeling sock | | 8 |
| 1909 Jan 19 | To laying sock | 1 | 6 |
| 29 | To steeling sock and laying coulter | 1 | 8 |
| 30 | To 4 new shoes mare | 3 | |
| | | 3 | 2 |

Paid 10/2/09
Henry Cargo

Fig 14 Invoice, Henry Cargo of the Inch, 1908-1909 (DB 111 DCM 1990-9/1).

## 4. Valuation of land, farm machinery and furniture, 1890 (Fig 15).

| | |
|---|---|
| 11 Acres Irish Wheat | £50: 0: 0. |
| 13 Do. Oats | 50: 0: 0 |
| 7 Do. Potatoes | 28: 0: 0 |
| 4 Do. Turnips | 4: 0: 0 |
| 8 tons Hay | 16: 0: 0 |
| 15 cwt. Straw | 1: 0: 0 |
| 6 Horses | 70: 0: 0 |
| 8 Cows | 64: 0: 0 |
| 2 two year-old heifers | 18: 0: 0 |
| 13 yearlings | 52: 0: 0 |
| 22 Calves | 30: 0: 0 |
| 7 Pigs (Shots) | 10: 0: 0 |
| 1 Sow | 3: 0: 0 |
| 1 threshing Machine | 6: 0: 0 |
| 1 pair of Fanners | 1: 10: 0 |
| 1 Churning Machine | 3: 0: 0 |
| 1 reaping Machine | 9: 0: 0 |
| 2 Ploughs | 1: 0: 0 |
| 2 pair of harrows, | 1: 0: 0 |
| 1 horse rake | 1:10: 0 |
| 1 Roller | 5: 0 |
| 1 drill harrow | 5: 0 |
| 1 Grubber | 5: 0 |
| 3 Carts | 6: 0: 0 |
| 1 Gaunting Car | 5: 0: 0 |
| Farming Tools, | 15: 0 |
| Manure, | 2: 0: 0 |
| Plough and Cart Harness | 2: 0: 0 |
| Furniture, | 6: 0: 0 |
| Farms as per separate Valuation | 792: 0: 0 |

Fig 15a Valuation of land, equipment and furniture, 1890, Page 1 (DB 1145 DCM 2008-152).

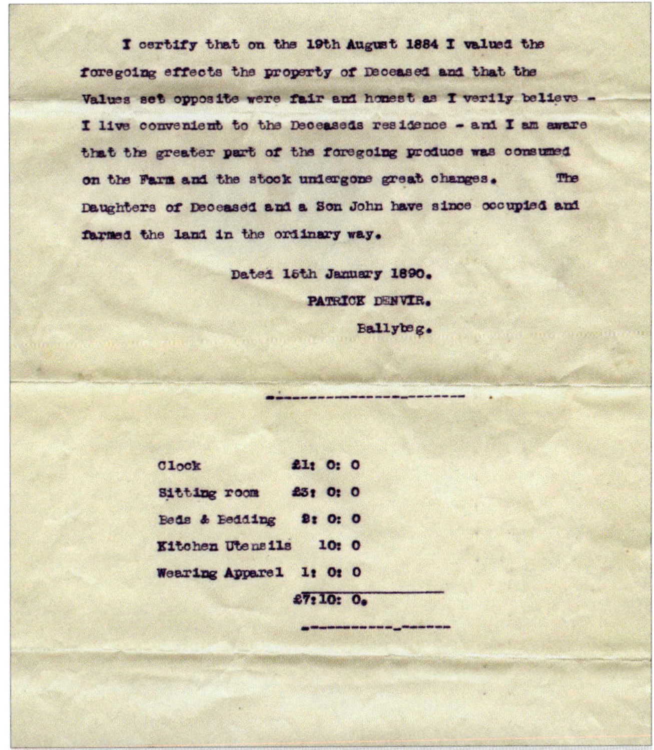

I certify that on the 19th August 1884 I valued the foregoing effects the property of Deceased and that the Values set opposite were fair and honest as I verily believe - I live convenient to the Deceaseds residence - and I am aware that the greater part of the foregoing produce was consumed on the Farm and the stock undergone great changes. The Daughters of Deceased and a Son John have since occupied and farmed the land in the ordinary way.

Dated 15th January 1890.
PATRICK DENVIR,
Ballybeg.

---

| | |
|---|---|
| Clock | £1: 0: 0 |
| Sitting room | £3: 0: 0 |
| Beds & Bedding | 2: 0: 0 |
| Kitchen Utensils | 10: 0 |
| Wearing Apparel | 1: 0: 0 |
| | £7:10: 0. |

Fig 15b Valuation of land, equipment and furniture, 1890, Page 2 (DB 1145 DCM 2008-152).

**5. Invoice for Ferguson tractor, 1936** (Fig 16).
This document, and the valuation illustrated on p105, came from the Denvir farm at Ballybeg, Downpatrick. The invoice, along with others for implements and replacement tractors in succeeding years, demonstrates how advanced the Denvir brothers were. Other documents in this donation include an estate map, farm accounts and instruction leaflets, especially relating to the Ferguson System.
*Given by Mr Alfie Linehan, Ardmeen, Downpatrick.*
DB 1144 DCM 2008-144 and 152

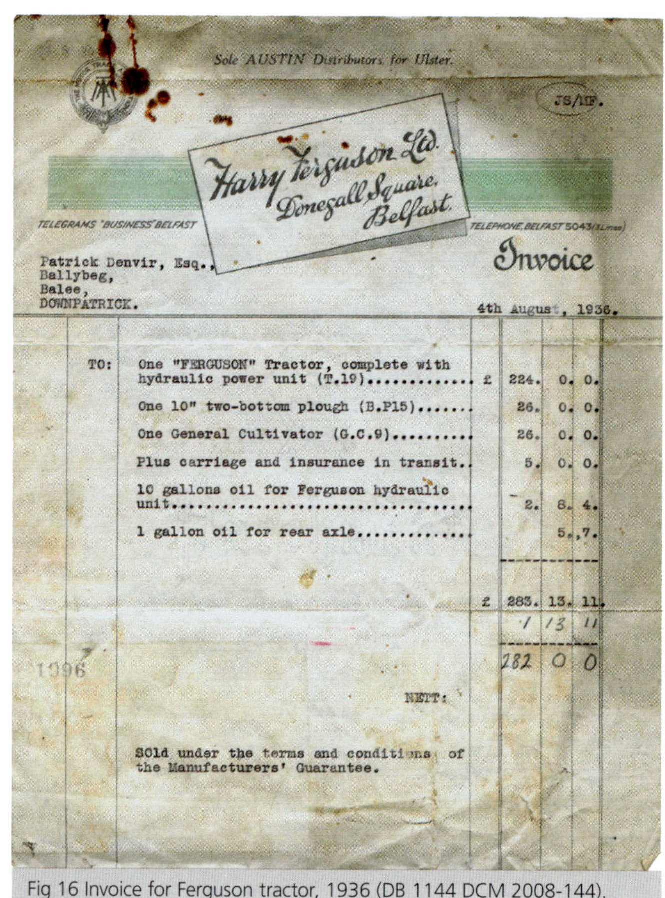

Sole AUSTIN Distributors for Ulster.

JS/MF.

Harry Ferguson Ltd.
Donegall Square,
Belfast.

TELEGRAMS "BUSINESS" BELFAST

TELEPHONE, BELFAST 5043 (3 Lines)

Invoice

Patrick Denvir, Esq.,
Ballybeg,
Balee,
DOWNPATRICK.

4th August, 1936.

| | | | £ | s. | d. |
|---|---|---|---|---|---|
| TO: | One "FERGUSON" Tractor, complete with hydraulic power unit (T.19)............ | £ | 224. | 0. | 0. |
| | One 10" two-bottom plough (B.P15)....... | | 26. | 0. | 0. |
| | One General Cultivator (G.C.9).......... | | 26. | 0. | 0. |
| | Plus carriage and insurance in transit.. | | 5. | 0. | 0. |
| | 10 gallons oil for Ferguson hydraulic unit.................................. | | 2. | 8. | 4. |
| | 1 gallon oil for rear axle............. | | | 5. | 7. |
| | | £ | 283. | 13. | 11. |
| | | | 1 | 13 | 11 |
| 1996 | | | 282 | 0 | 0 |
| | NETT: | | | | |

SOld under the terms and conditions of the Manufacturers' Guarantee.

Fig 16 Invoice for Ferguson tractor, 1936 (DB 1144 DCM 2008-144).

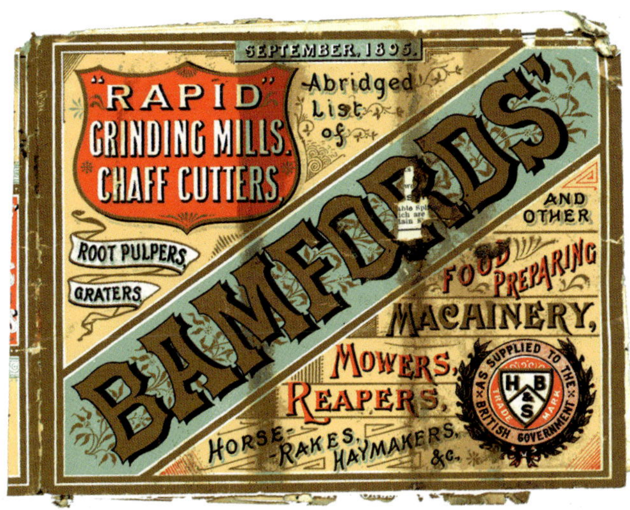


Fig 17 Bamford's catalogue, 1895 (DB 332 DCM 1996-218).

**6. Catalogue, Bamfords' agricultural implements, 1895** (Fig 17).
This was found behind a dresser in the donor's house during renovation work.
*Given by Ms M Lesley Simpson, Balloo, Killinchy.*
DB 332 DCM 1996-218

# CHAPTER 5

## Agricultural prize medals of the nineteenth century

Robert Heslip

Prize medals probably developed from the presentation of high value coins, sometimes specially produced for the purpose of rewards. The idea of premiums (the concept survives in common use with 'premium bonds') as a tool became popular in the eighteenth century. Usually these were grants of money to encourage innovation or good practice, but there was sometimes a feeling that gentlemen could not accept cash. There was no social opprobrium, however. attached to accepting medals given as a way of recognising achievement. Some medals could have considerable financial value and there was nothing to stop both sorts of reward being used together.

In Ireland, the Dublin Society (with the title 'Royal' from 1820) was set up in 1731 by a group of people keen to encourage advances in arts, industry, science and agriculture. From 1741 premiums targeted specific areas of concern, among which good farming practice was prominent. Medals started to be issued from the 1760s as another way of recognising achievement. Ireland was in the European vanguard in this proactive encouragement, but interest in new farming methods – ranging across cultivation, animal breeds and machinery – became more widespread across the British Isles (and further afield) as the eighteenth century progressed. This interest resulted in a number of farming societies appearing, including in 1800 a Farming Society of Ireland, as well as others organised on a county (including Down) or more local basis. These do not seem to have had much of an impact, perhaps because they lacked the will or capacity to engage with the huge number of small tenant farmers who were responsible for the bulk of food production. The Farming Society of Ireland was incorporated in 1815, and received a government grant of £5000 a year, but seems to have stopped operations by 1828. In the north of Ireland, North East and North West Farming Associations were established in 1821 and for a time both were very active, holding well supported shows and, in the case of the North West, establishing a progressive agricultural school at Templemoyle which was recognised as a valuable development model. Neither lasted, however, but the North East Association was revived as the North East Agricultural Society after a meeting in Hillsborough in 1854. This continues to flourish today as the Royal Ulster Agricultural Society.

The source of most Irish agricultural medals, and the context of those in the museum collection belong to a different and quite specific stage. This was signalled by the establishment of the Agricultural Improvement Association of Ireland in 1841. The organisation lasted more than forty years, acquiring a 'royal' prefix along the way, and a further change of name in 1860 to the Royal Agricultural Society of Ireland. In a pleasingly circular manner, part of its role was taken over when it was absorbed by the Royal Dublin Society in 1887, later augmented by a government Department of Agricultural and Technical Instruction in 1900.

Perceptions of Irish agriculture in the nineteenth century are inevitably dominated by the Great Famine. Cataclysmic as this was, by definition it affected only one crop, in a relatively concentrated period. Almost all land was owned by a small number of wealthy landowners, who in many cases were eager to maximise the return from their capital asset. From the 1820s, interest in improving the productivity of animals, the selection of crop varieties to increase yields, experimentation with fertilisers and cultivation techniques – lazy beds seem to have been regarded with particular disdain – and technology grew both from economic self-interest and more general aspirations connected to ideas of progress and philanthropy. The need to respond to the accelerating movement of population from the country to industrialising towns was a further contributing factor, though this was much slower to happen in Ireland than in England. Cyclical economic pressures were also important and provided both threats and opportunities in terms of change. Local conditions led to a special enthusiasm for drainage. Individual polemicists urged the adoption of particular systems, but perhaps the biggest change was the industrial production of pottery land drains. These factors came together in what was termed 'thorough drainage' which had the potential to have a huge influence on productivity. The technique was singled out early by the Royal Agricultural Improvement Society through publications, premiums and the award of prize medals. Whether or not the Society's encouragement had a large impact, the Irish landscape was transformed during the period. Vast areas of wetland or bog designated in the 1830s on the first six-inch-to-the-mile scale Ordnance Survey maps disappear from subsequent editions in a way that makes some landscapes hardly recognisable.

The Royal Agricultural Improvement Society of Ireland (RAISI) was an interesting model, operating on a national level, but recognising the importance of local action, mainly through the medium of local farming societies. Its influence meant that numbers of societies increased substantially, probably peaking in the 1840s and then declining from the 1850s, before reviving again under the twin stimulae of renewed technical change, including the widespread adoption of machinery for the first time, and the Land Purchase Acts, which finally transferred farm ownership to tenants, and with it the incentive to invest and improve.

The RAISI's objectives included holding a national cattle show; the establishment of local farming societies to which premiums could be given for the improvement and encouragement of stock, green crops and thorough drainage. It also had a series of rules for affiliated societies, such as that none would be entitled to premiums unless at least five members were also members and annual subscribers to the central body, or a sum equivalent to at least six annual subscriptions of £1 were paid. Rule 4 is particularly interesting - *That money premiums be confined exclusively to working farmers living principally by husbandry and holding not more than 20 acres statute measure and residing within the limits of each local society.*[1] This, of course, did not exclude larger farmers and landowners from receiving the prize medals and it is probable that these more prosperous individuals are disproportionately represented among surviving medals, especially for livestock.

County Down tops the list for numbers of affiliated farming societies – not all local societies were necessarily affiliated - but it is safe to presume that the vast majority took advantage of the benefits the connection offered. There were twelve listed for the county in 1848, out of an all-Ireland total of 109 – just over 11%[2]. Antrim had the next highest total of any county, after Down, with 11 societies. It is probably safe to take the presence of farming societies as an indication of active interest in agricultural improvement and a likely high standard of farming practice. Better economic conditions and landlord-tenant relations across areas of Ulster, compared to other areas, is reflected in the fact that the number of societies reached 40 in the province.

Most local farming societies did not go to the expense of having their own medals produced, even from stock dies, but had the generic Royal Agricultural Improvement Society medal engraved with their own name and that of the recipient. Given the variety of styles used, this was almost certainly done locally. It was not uncommon for the awarding society's name to be engraved on the edge and the name of the recipient across the blank space in the middle of the reverse. The reason for the award is not always included, but interestingly, the place, usually a townland, is almost always given.

Coins and medals have two faces designated – the obverse and the reverse – equivalent to 'heads and tails' in popular usage referring to coins. The terms have a technical and functional significance, relating to the production process. Most medals are made by striking between dies – lumps of steel with the design on the working face. The lower one is fixed, and wears more slowly than the upper one which moves down with great force on the disk of metal to press the design on both sides of the finished object. As the lower die lasts much longer than the upper, it is worth spending more time on the design, which also tends to be in higher relief. For earlier RAISI medals an obverse design heavily laden with significance and symbolism was chosen (Fig 1). It is signed with *Lizars INV. Ingram. SC.* Lizars were an Edinburgh-based firm of engravers on steel – including banknote printing plates. The abbreviations stand for Invenit which can be translated from the Latin as 'designed by' and Sculptit 'engraved by'. The main figure is Hibernia[3], the female personification of Ireland, using a laurel wreath to crown a young man with her right hand. The laurel wreath was the classical symbol of victory and was used to celebrate the winners in motor sport until quite recently. Hibernia's left arm rests on a large harp with a discreetly small crown. The rest of the scene is crammed, slightly randomly, with things representing a range of agricultural activity. The young man, while leaning on an improved plough with an iron share, also holds a reaping hook. Behind him is a sheaf of corn. A ewe and lamb to the left look disproportionately small in comparison to a very fine cow. All this is of general agricultural interest rather than relating specifically to Ireland.

The reverse, struck by the upper die, is much more simple. The title of the society and its date of foundation run outside a shamrock wreath and large central blank space in which engraving could be placed.

This design of medal was replaced in the 1850s by a larger, but more simply designed medal, represented here by an award of the Lecale Farming Society (Fig 2). The

Fig 1 Medal awarded by the Royal Agricultural Improvement Society of Ireland to James Morrow of Feeny, 1845, for the greatest quantity of thorough draining in the Dromore Farming Society, 44mm diam (DB 17 DCM 1985-8). The museum has two more medals awarded by this Society. One was awarded to James Morrow of Ballynagarahan for the best cultivated root crop in the Dromore Farming Society (DB 17 DCM 1985-9). The other was awarded to John Davidson of Drumaness (DB 1081 DCM 2004-201).

Fig 2 Medal awarded by the Lecale Farming Society to John Waring Maxwell of Finnebrogue for the best bull, 51mm diam (DB 836 DCM 1998-66).

obverse features a large harp, which contrasts with the earlier version. The first type is an awkward combination of a half-understood Gaelic harp and the concert harp which was popular for drawing room entertainment as well as formal performance, but the revision shows a clear awareness of the Celtic Revival and actual Irish harps. The crown is more prominent, but still smaller than that used by most government-connected organisations. The same text is used, but perhaps arranged with more design consciousness. The medallist this time was Dublin-based, a man called Jones, who was also responsible for a number of contemporary Orange pieces. The reverse has a complex wreath using palm, laurel and oak, the first two types of leaf with symbolism related directly to victory, the third relating to citizenship, strength and loyalty. The wreath leaves space outside for the name of the farming society as well as room inside for the details of the award.

Over time the Agricultural Improvement Society became less active. The total premiums plummeted from £3843 in 1841 to £843 in 1849 and continued to fall. Part of this was undoubtedly due to the Famine, but later the influence of the Land League and Land War probably had a greater effect. The Royal Dublin Society did not attempt to work at a local level to the same degree and many of the weaker societies disappeared, leaving a smaller number of stronger, locally-based, organisations. These had to find their own medals and most turned to stock designs from England. As already discussed, the obverse die was the important, expensive element of the production. This is demonstrated very well by the medal of the Newry Union Farming Society[4] (Fig 3). The obverse is signed by Ottley of Birmingham, who was a competent, if undistinguished, medallist. The scene depicted is clearly English, judging by the house in the background. An attempt is made to cover as many sorts of farm livestock as possible, with a horse, a bull, a cow with long horns, a ewe and a pig as well as a range of poultry, one of which is shown in sufficient detail to suggest a Polish (referring to the 'poll', rather than ethnicity) rooster. By this stage medal dies tended to be made up of a series of standard elements – such as the wreath – and the name of the society would have been easily, and cheaply, added with letter punches.

Fig 3 Medal awarded by the Newry Union Farming Society to the Rt Hon Earl Kilmorey, for Filly Rose, 1880, 47mm diam (DB 1074 DCM 2004-167).

The same is true of the medal of the Killyleagh, Killinchy, Kilmood and Tullynakill Farming Society, signed by the Birmingham firm of Allen and Moore (Fig 4). Much of their production was at the cheaper end of the market, such as souvenir and school medals. The cottage is clearly of English style, as is the dress of the ploughman. The most prominent feature of the background, however, is universal – a rising sun to symbolise hope and renewal. In this specimen the reverse consists solely of a fairly plain laurel wreath, with a large blank space across which details of the award could be engraved. It seems that often this was left up to the recipient, who sometimes either did not get round to having the work done, or did not consider it worth the cost.

As the nineteenth century progressed into the twentieth, there was a change of fashion in agricultural prizes. While the medal has never disappeared, silver cups and other sorts of trophy became more popular. Part of the reason for this was a reinforcement of localism – cups were often provided through the personal donation of individuals for perpetual award, or only available for outright possession through a series of consecutive wins. More recently, commercial sponsorship has become important. Collections of the earlier agricultural medals provide valuable physical evidence for important phases of development, as well as aesthetically-pleasing examples of applied art and design.

Fig 4 Medal awarded by the Killyleagh,Killinchy, Kilmood and Tullynakill Farming Society, 44mm diam (DB 1081 DCM 2004-202).

**REFERENCES**


1. Thoms *Irish Almanac and General Directory 1848* (Dublin, 1847) p 288. Principally by husbandry is italicised in the original.

2. They are Ards, Bangor, Donaghmore, Dromore, Drumbo and Drumbeg (listed under Antrim), Holywood, Killyleagh and Killinchy *sic*, Lecale, Mourne and Killowen, Newtownards, Saintfield and Kilmore, Seaforde and Hollymount. We can assume that the longer title of the Killyleagh society, as on the last medal discussed here, was abbreviated simply in the interests of saving space in a double-column format.

3. There is a different female personification on Royal Dublin Society medals, often assumed to be Hibernia, but who is in fact Minerva, dispensing prosperity from an upturned cornucopia.

4. Part of the RAISI regulations was that farming societies should be based on Poor Law Union districts.